Here lyeth the Body . . .

A look at Worcestershire churchyards

by

Sam Redgrave

 Halfshire Books

Halfshire Books
6 High Street, Bromsgrove
Worcestershire B61 8HQ

First published in Great Britain
by Halfshire Books 1992

ISBN 0 9513525 6 3

Typeset in Great Britain by Avon Dataset,
Bidford-on-Avon and printed in Great Britain
by BPCC Wheatons Ltd, Exeter

Would ye find out a fitting tomb? These firs,
Their sea-like dirge soft whispering day and night,
Hither your weary wandering steps invite:
These yew trees' massive shade, that hardly stirs
On the grey tomb-stones.
All the still churchyard,
Not mingling with the haunts of men yet seen
(As if just so much of the world is shared
As might wake Charity and silence Pride);
Come take your rest with those by Holy Hammond's side.

(Lines from a sonnet by John Keble, written after a pilgrimage in 1819 to the grave of Henry Hammond, distinguished theologian and chaplain to Charles I, who is buried at Hampton Lovett.)

Acknowledgements

A number of people have been helpful in the preparation of this book but particular thanks are due to Vivian Bird for help with the Upton Warren conundrum; Peter Bright, stonemason at Bromsgrove; Rev Peter Emerson and some of his parishioners in Wychbold; Tony Higgs, Secretary of the Worcester Diocesan Advisory Committee; Ted Payne, Chairman of the Properties Committee, St Peter de Witton, Droitwich; Peter Wardle of Bayton; and Anne Whiting of Hampton Lovett.

Illustrations

Cover and line drawings by Judy Hadley

Photographs by Nick Trow except those on pages 64 and 90 by Max Harper and on pages 2, 6, 7, 27, 33, 48, 68, 84, 92, 104, 110 and 117 which are from the author's own collection

Contents

Introduction

To the ever dear memory of PERCY EATON who was killed on the Honeybourne Cricket Field August 18th 1908 in his 27th year.

Churchyards have been a prominent feature of our landscape for hundreds of years, a part of our country's way of life. A church without a churchyard looks and feels incomplete, like a fish out of water. So for that matter does a church with a churchyard that has been completely cleared of its memorials: it looks decidedly two-dimensional. The church needs a setting and the age-old setting in England has been 'God's Acre', the grassy area dotted with tombs and gravestones which marks the physical ending of men, women and children, most of whom until comparatively recently would have been baptised and married in the same place.

Asked to conjure up in the mind's eye a picture of an old English churchyard most would imagine an area around a stone church, entered by a lychgate, usually of wood, often intricately carved, with tombs and headstones of all shapes and sizes standing higgledy-piggledy in the grass and telling something of the history of the area and its people over the previous three or four centuries. Some would go further and add to this picture a churchyard cross, a sundial perhaps, ancient yews, wild flowers of spring and summer and the lichen and moss that cover the stones, the brambles and creepers that hold them in their grip.

   In contrast the imagined municipal cemetery would present a
quite different picture — neat, uniform, monotonous even,
nothing of the wild beauty that is characteristic of so many
churchyards or the Gothic gloom that can envelop some of them
in winter, nowhere near as packed with history, with few of the
quirky, tantalising or fulsome epitaphs which can be read
around the churchyard. There are of course exceptions and the
cemetery at Bromsgrove is one of them, with its pleasant setting,
beautiful trees and interesting nineteenth- and twentieth-century
memorials. It was a rather glorious exception from the start
when an article in *The Civil Engineer and Architects' Journal* in
1858 singled it out as very finely and appropriately designed, 'an
ornament to the town'. But almost always it is the churchyard,
where nature is allowed to flourish, that proves the more
enticing.

Ankle-twisting country: part of the
large churchyard at Inkberrow

And there are some striking examples of the triumph of nature in the county's two hundred churchyards. The older part of the extensive churchyard at Inkberrow would take the prize for the best example of ankle-twisting country with grasses and cow parsley shoulder- and gravestone-high. At Rous Lench a great old tree stump, grasses and flowers in attendance, has been allowed space to become an attractive feature at the west end of the church. At Huddington roots have been creeping out of a vault like gnarled many-fingered hands, breaking up the tombstone of William Gerrard; at Romsley a tree has bent under the weight of a sinking stone, only to straighten out above it to show who is the winner. The waving arms of ivy, creeper and bramble, blown by the wind off the taller stones, must have been the stuff of many a Worcestershire ghost story; and the creaking of tall trees — try walking up the path to the porch at Feckenham in the dark — can accentuate the 'other worldliness' of these places.

Worcestershire has many beautiful churchyards with wonderful views over the surrounding countryside, among them Bayton, sited on a hilltop near the Shropshire border with fine views over the valley between Tenbury and the Clee Hills; Lindridge, perched on a hill above the road, looking down over the fruit orchards to the River Teme; Abberley with woods and hills to the south and south-east of the younger of the two churchyards; and in the north of the county arguably the two best sited of all: Tardebigge, church and churchyard crowning the hill, the canal at the bottom and wonderful views to the north, and Hanbury, a magnificent vantage point at the top of this wooded mound offering panoramic views which extend, on a clear day, as far as Bredon and the Cotswolds.

This book then sets out to discover something of the variety of churchyards in this beautiful county, the light they shed on the past and the kinds of tombs and headstones they house. In the process it looks at a wide range of epitaphs, those final comments on our ancestors that can sometimes tell all (perhaps more than we need to know), and sometimes not enough — we want more. Whose interest could fail to be aroused by the opening epitaph, for instance? Who was Percy Eaton? And how exactly was he killed? By a ball? By lightning? Or something more bizarre? In Ribbesford, near Bewdley, there are several nineteenth-century headstones which refer to the United Ancient Order of Druids whose lodges met at various inns in the town. But what kind of an organisation was it? Most mysterious of all perhaps is the stone at Wychbold in memory of 'fifty infants gathered unto their Saviour's bosom'. There are no details and no date. Who were the children? How and when did they die? Churchyards provide wonderful food for speculation.

Most epitaphs however are straightforward enough, brief summaries of reasonably normal and uneventful lives. But even these cannot always be taken at face value. On his tomb George Nicholson of Stourport is described as an honest and warm human being, devoted to the cause of literature. He very probably was. But nothing is said about the revolutionary trend in book production he started, a style soon copied by the big booksellers in London. At the northern edge of the churchyard at Hanbury is a slightly curious but very plain monument to Emma Phillips, daughter and heiress of Thomas Vernon of Hanbury Hall. Only the words 'and was by her own desire buried here', in an otherwise straightforwardly brief epitaph, would alert the passer-by to the possibility of scandal — or some other drama that resulted in her body being laid to rest here rather than in the Vernon family vault.

Searching for unusual epitaphs and gravestones is an age-old pastime and Worcestershire can be grateful to people like John Noake who began recording a number of more unusual ones nearly one hundred and fifty years ago, many of which have since disappeared. It was clearly a highly popular recreation a century ago, too — though not with everyone:

Harris wanted to get out at Hampton Church, to go and see Mrs Thomas's tomb.

'Who is Mrs Thomas?' I asked.

'How should I know?' replied Harris. 'She's a lady that's got a funny tomb, and I want to see it.'

I objected. I don't know whether it is that I am built wrong, but I never did seem to hanker after tombstones myself. I know that the proper thing to do, when you get to a village or town, is to rush off to the churchyard, and enjoy the graves ... I shock respectable sextons by the imperturbability I am able to assume before exciting inscriptions, and by my lack of enthusiasm for the local family history ... Harris, however, revels in tombs, and graves, and epitaphs, and monumental inscriptions ... He said he had looked forward to seeing Mrs Thomas's grave from the first moment that the trip was proposed — said he wouldn't have joined if it hadn't been for the idea of seeing Mrs Thomas's tomb.

Jerome K Jerome *Three Men in a Boat* (1889)

The author of this book has kept strictly to the churchyard. (Not true, of course, but where he has strayed into the church he has kept his notes to himself.) Church memorials of Worcestershire would be worthy of another book for there are some very fine ones indeed: at Cropthorne, for example, where Francis Dingley, his wife and nineteen children have rested in painted splendour for nearly four hundred years, while his grandson's family are buried nearby in an equally beautiful tomb; at Wickhamford which houses two magnificent seventeenth-century monuments to the Sandys family; and at St Peter de Witton in Droitwich where lawyer Wylde, Lord Chief Baron of the Exchequer under Thomas Cromwell, opulent and sombre, has slept for four hundred years.

Not all burial grounds are Anglican, of course. Other denominations have had their own burial places for centuries, the oldest probably those belonging to the Quakers. The rise of

A variety of gravestones at Chaddesley Corbett

the nonconformists and the building of Roman Catholic churches in the last century meant there were chapels and meeting houses dotted all round Worcestershire and in keeping with the principle that the churchyard represents the living *and* the dead church some established their own burial grounds. In towns these could be quite sizable but in villages many were quite small, reflecting their smaller congregations, among the exceptions the Baptist burial ground at Atch Lench, over 150 years old and unusually large, the former Baptist chapel at Bengeworth where the eighteenth-century graveyard was also quite substantial, the Roman Catholic burial ground of St Benet's at Kemerton, and the burial ground in front of the Unitarian chapel in Evesham, one of the most attractive nonconformist buildings in the county.

Sadly, so many dissenting churches have gone, sometimes rebuilt on the same site, more often pulled down to enable congregations to regroup more realistically; and so the buildings and, where they existed, burial grounds lie under car parks, supermarkets, housing estates and, in at least one instance until recently, under a billiard hall. In the few existing non-Anglican burial grounds the memorials vary from the extremely simple, bearing only a name and a date (usually belonging to the Quakers who eschewed any hint of ornament and display), to the mildly flamboyant, surprising in view of the simplicity which characterises most nonconformist buildings.

Approaching graveyards requires some sensitivity. They are after all the resting places of the dead and, as such, areas which hold memories important to the living. It is good to remember this, since the redigging and reuse of graves means that relatively recent graves can often be located among others so old that their families have long ceased to visit. St George's, Kidderminster, and St James in West Malvern, for instance, have alongside graves of the last century those of the past twenty years; and a figure bending to read a nearby headstone in the old

The lychgate at Overbury, a war memorial in the centre

part of Ribbesford churchyard was not on a general 'Harris' visit
but gazing at the grave of his mother, dead some forty years. He
was one of the group of people who most regularly visit our
churchyards, those who go to tend graves or simply to remember
in a few minutes solitude the relatives or friends buried there.

But there are many others who visit churchyards for different
reasons. As well as the keen epitaph-seekers — kneeling to squint
at indecipherable lettering, bent double in an effort to get at the
face of the stone now buried under trees — there are those
interested in the grasses, wild flowers and lichen rarely seen
beyond the boundary walls; in the craftsmanship that has gone
into the memorials themselves, the carving and lettering, the
shaping of the stone; and others intent only on a quiet stroll
through a bit of land shared by man and nature for hundreds of
years. Not that it is always that peaceful, of course. The noises
coming from an adjoining field of sheep one afternoon in early
spring at little out-of-the-way Rushock could not have sounded
more like a group of actors hamming it up.

There are also those whose main target is the church, the
churchyard only an incidental. Sadly, but understandably,
increased vandalism has led to the locking of so many churches
(a good half of Worcestershire's churches were locked in 1992).
But there's little new under the sun. A century and a half ago
John Noake didn't always find churches open either. When he
visited Stockton-on-Teme he was relieved to find the door
'invitingly open' and 'pleased that so good and primitive a
practice' was still observed. It was not a new problem then for
Noake quotes from a poetical satire by Horace Smith:

> *If, with diurnal drudgeries o'erwrought,*
> *Or sick of dissipation's dull vagaries,*
> *We wish to snatch one little space for thought,*
> *Or holy respite, in our sanctuaries;*
> *Why are they shut?*   ....

If there be one — one only — who might share
This sanctifying week-day adoration,
Were but our churches open to his prayer,
Why — I demand with earnest iteration —
Why are they shut?

Rejected Addresses

Perhaps would-be visitors to churches will be spending a little more time in churchyards in future. They will rarely be disappointed. A great many of God's Acres (and there are some 12,000 in England and Wales) are little oases of land hardly touched by the great changes to agriculture during the past two centuries. Consequently they play a major role in providing food and shelter for birds, insects and small animals, including cats. Cat-lovers may reap an unexpected bonus for the churchyard cats of Worcestershire are a truly wonderful bunch. In Mathon, right on the border, he was handsome, black, dignified and immaculately-mannered, ready and waiting in the car park, providing an escort across the road and through the churchyard, discreetly finding things to do until the visit was over when he reappeared near the porch (containing his picture and a polite request to make sure he was not left in the church), showed the way back and watched serenely as the car moved off. In Dodderhill the resident host was a beautiful marmalade-and-white creature, friendly, pretty-faced and gloriously bushy-tailed. In Knighton-on-Teme the sparkling little tabby was definitely female, delighted to have some company, bosom pal within seconds, sticking close throughout, accompanying her latest fan back to the car and, a final performance, rolling over in a cowpat.

I Four hundred years of marking the spot

The origin of the Christian burial ground is still not crystal clear. Its establishment is normally attributed to Cuthbert, Archbishop of Canterbury, who obtained approval from Rome in the eighth century to set up churchyards around churches in big centres of population in the hope that this would prompt churchgoers to pray for the souls of the buried ones and remind them of their own mortality. Most of our churchyards date back to the tenth century, though in the West Midlands and South-East England some are much older, established at the dawn of British Christianity; and because the first churches were very often built of wood — and therefore perished — many churchyards are older than the stone churches they surround.

A few Saxon and medieval churchyard monuments have survived but most of these either lie buried beneath the soil and grass, from time to time exposed by gravedigging and repairs; or they have been taken into churches or museums for protection. In 1860 St Mary's, Tenbury, was undergoing major restoration and when part of the chancel wall was pulled down a fragment of an Anglo-Saxon preaching cross was discovered, about two feet in size and carved on all four sides. Now it stands inside the church protected by glass; once it would have stood in the churchyard, a rallying point for the faithful. Another of the county's treasures was also unearthed from a chancel wall — a finely carved head of an Anglo-Saxon cross which came to light in the eighteenth century at St Michael's, Cropthorne. It dates back to the very early ninth century and, unless it is on exhibition elsewhere, can be seen in all its intricate beauty inside the church.

The churchyard as we know it today dates largely from the end of the sixteenth century when the rise of a prosperous middle class led to the demand for some sort of monuments to mark the resting places of those who could now afford them. The most wealthy and important people in the parish continued wherever possible to be buried and erect their memorials inside the church as they had always done; while the overwhelming majority of people went on being buried without any tomb, stone or proper marker to indicate the spot, the fate of many of the poor well into the last century. It's hard, for example, to find memorial stones to those bottom-of-the-heap workers, the nailers of North Worcestershire, and when John Noake visited Wyre Piddle in the mid-nineteenth century he found that the majority of burials were marked only by pegs driven into the ground and numbered — and clearly shuddered at the practice, fervently hoping that his remains would not be 'ticketed and labelled, like a lot in an auctioneer's catalogue or a prize pig at an agricultural show'.

But in between these two groups was the burgeoning middle class — merchants, skilled craftsmen, yeoman farmers — and outside on the grassy area around the church their memorials began to sprout, short and dumpy, epitaphs brief and to the point, usually stone, sometimes of wood. Examples of these earlier gravestones are increasingly rare: for the most part our

A simple early headstone at Upton Warren. Note the joined capitals

knowledge of late sixteenth-century memorials comes from written records, particularly the books and articles of earlier local historians.

Noake, for example, seems to have covered (largely on foot) practically every blade of grass in Worcestershire, describing each churchyard in general and those memorials in particular that he found most interesting. The Cotton brothers, John and William, concentrated their local history investigations on the Bromsgrove area. All three were well aware of what had already been lost in the churchyard. Noake quotes a number of examples of memorials referred to by earlier writers but no longer there in his time and William Cotton, lamenting the way so many of the older stones had been moved from their original position to support the banks along the paths, makes it clear that at one time St John's had had at least a few headstones from the 1500s. It still has a fine collection of seventeenth-century headstones in varying degrees of completeness and readability and there are good seventeenth-century examples at Bretforton, Broadway, Cleeve Prior, Harvington, near Evesham, and Norton and Lenchwick. The lettering on these early monuments was often crude, the layout primitive and the level of literacy fairly low, but there is a vigour and an individual home-made quality about the work that proves extremely attractive.

In most churchyards, however, the oldest monuments are from the eighteenth century and the spread of wealth and taste as that century advanced can be seen very clearly in Worcestershire. Tombs are fashioned with greater skill and appreciation of design — baroque, rococo, neo-classical — some of superb quality; and the earlier rustic lettering gives way to the skilled use of the Roman alphabet and more individual styles. At Ashton-under-Hill a group of headstones to members of the Proctor family (especially the one to Ann Proctor who died in

Ann Proctor's headstone at Ashton-under-Hill

1797) shows a very high standard of lettering. In fact several
other village churchyards around Bredon have eighteenth-
century headstones displaying similarly fine incised lettering.
Perhaps the work of the same mason.

Headstones, now much larger, begin to slim down from the
massively thick — anything up to 9 or 10 inches (22 to 25
centimetres); and there are many excellent examples of these in
Worcestershire churchyards, the one just to the left of the
church porch at Huddington as good as any. At the end of the
century they can still be quite solid, 5 or 6 inches, but within a
few years they are usually 3 inches or less. The characteristic
shape of the tops of the headstones — like a horizontal figure 3
— gradually disappears in favour of other shapes: curved,
indented, sometimes scrolled; and the increased skill of the
mason can be seen in the relief symbols and patterns worked on
the stone.

The years between 1750 and 1850 were the English
churchyard's greatest era: form and masonic talent combined to
produce a flood of well-designed memorials. It was also the
churchyard's last truly local age. The men who made the early
tombstones were local masons, carrying out all sorts of general
building and repair work mainly on non-religious buildings, a
situation which still held in some areas until comparatively
recently. By the end of the eighteenth century the specialised
trade of monumental masonry had evolved, largely rural-based
and always using local stone where available since the cost of
transporting the raw material in the pre-canal, pre-railway age
was prohibitive. Up until the middle of the last century,
therefore, Worcestershire churchyards were full of memorials
carved by local men from local stone on behalf of the families of
local people:

> And close by the church-yard, there's a stonemason's yard,
> that when the time is seasonable

Will furnish with affections sore and marble urns and cherubims
very low and reasonable.

Thomas Hood Our Village

The improvement in the transport system and the effects of the Industrial Revolution changed all that. Cheaper movement of people and goods led to the rapid spread of set monumental designs right across the country, mass-produced gravestones and monuments manufactured according to the specifications of respectable architects, chosen from trade catalogues. Masons only needed to cut out the inscriptions — and even these became less individual as people turned to epitaphs devised by a small band of 'writers' now making their living out of final words (some of these pretty excruciating and sickly — but probably no worse than much of the verse on today's greeting cards). Many village masons survived all this and continued to work to their own designs in local stone; but the great crop of new shapes and

A typically massive eighteenth-century stone at Upton Warren

materials, the inevitable result of industrialisation, is obvious
even to the most casual stroller through the county's
churchyards.

Our nineteenth-century forbears, however, faced a problem
far more urgent than the decline of individual craftsmanship.
The population explosion of the early decades together with
high birth and death rates — when medical progress simply
could not cope with the effects of poor sanitation, slums and
excessive drinking — put tremendous pressure on burial space;
and the state of English churchyards, more especially in the
towns and cities, became a cause of great alarm. The most awful
smells resulted from the piling of bodies on top of each other in
what we would now call shallow graves and the practice, until
the 1830s, of placing a slab on the grave to deter bodysnatchers
also unfortunately inhibited decomposition.

Cotton, writing about earlier times in the last century, gives
some idea of what a busy churchyard, St John's in Bromsgrove,
must have been like. Burials used to take place at the end of the
Sunday afternoon service and on one occasion there were eleven
coffins of various sizes lined up on forms in the middle of the
church until the service had finished. In Worcester, according to
Noake, the situation had become intolerable, most of the church
crypts full of rotting coffins and unburied bodies; and this was
not confined to urban areas: there were endless complaints from
rural communities about the condition of churchyards and the
bodies and mouldering bones in the vaults below the churches.
But these latter were much more to do with the long neglect of
church and churchyard and the general lowering of burial
standards than with any dramatic increase in village population.

A graphic example of these problems is outlined in the guide
to St Peter's, Inkberrow, which may have been built on a former
pagan burial site. Christian burials have been taking place at
Inkberrow for at least 800 years, so that as many as 20,000
bodies could well have lain beneath the soil. Pressure on burial

space led to the churchyard's extension in 1857 (and again in 1945). But another problem stems from this long-term use of areas around churches: the level of the soil steadily rises over the centuries, so that the ground in the churchyard can end up several feet higher than the floor of the church and the road outside, creating tremendous drainage problems and leading, as it did at Inkberrow, to damp and mould inside the church. At St Peter's, as at many other churchyards, soil was removed to level the site and in the process many old tombs and headstones were destroyed or covered with grass.

The chronic situation was relieved by the establishment of public cemeteries — largely in built-up areas — and by the extension of churchyards in rural areas. Bromsgrove had already extended its old churchyard before the new cemetery was built in the late 1850s; and throughout the last thirty years extension has been going on in many Worcestershire village churchyards. The nation's concern may best be judged by the fact that between 1852 and 1906 there were no less than fifteen Acts of Parliament concerned with the business of burial.

It was a single event towards the end of the century, however, that heralded the practice which is rapidly becoming the norm and revolutionising the appearance of traditional English churchyards. The first official cremation took place in 1885 but because of widespread opposition it was another eighteen years before it was regularised. Now over 60% of us choose to be cremated and areas of the churchyard are paved with rows of small flat tablets, quite at odds with the appearance of the rest of the churchyard and the church itself. Perhaps, as the authors of *The Churchyard Handbook* suggest, the answer is to inter ashes in a clearly designated area but with no headstone; or to erect large headstones which will accommodate a number of inscriptions. These kinds of solutions are being worked out in churchyards like Rous Lench, Cropthorne, Overbury and Holt.

Whatever happens, it is clear that after some 400 years the old

English churchyard is itself coming to an end, its characteristic appearance eroded not only by cremation tablets but by the introduction of white marble, so un-English, and polished granite in its varied colours, and by mass production at its most monotonous. It is possible, of course, that at some point in the future — maybe the near future — no-one will be buried in the old way, that we will all have returned to the very ancient practice of cremation. There is increasing awareness that in the meantime there must be some real encouragement to produce memorials from individual designs and, where available, from local materials.

There have certainly been a few attempts in this century. Just outside the east end of St Eadburgha's, Broadway, is an attractive individually-designed memorial of appropriate stone to Edith Gill; at St Benet's, Kemerton, there is another modern simple headstone of grey slate, this one to Barbara Gwendoline Whittle, whose incised name and dates are painted in gold; and very striking are the unusually narrow and tall headstones at Norton and Lenchwick to Rev Walter Consitt Boulter, vicar at the turn of the century, and his wife, Hannah. Nearer to the churchyard entrance is a stylish Celtic cross-shaped headstone to the Boulters' daughter.

These and the few others which exist in Worcestershire show real commitment to design and the combination of originality and simplicity of line comes as a relief after the standardised fussiness of the previous decades. But the sad fact is that such headstones are now beyond the pocket of most people.

This diocese, like others, has introduced regulations aimed at encouraging good design and the use of local materials: acceptable dimensions of headstones, horizontal slab stones and simple crosses are clearly laid down, while some of the eyesores of recent decades just as clearly resisted. Headstones, the regulations explain, do not have to be rectangular — curved tops are preferable to straight-edged — but there is no place for stones

Rebekah Stanford died
Feb 15ᵗʰ 1784 Aged 82
Iohn Stanford Sen. died
Sep 28ᵗʰ 1785 Aged 93
Iohn Stanford Jun. died
Nov 10ᵗʰ 1783 Aged 48
Stanford die

Eighteenth-century elegance at Wickhamford

shaped as hearts or books, nor for kerbs and railings, chains and chippings round the base of the stone; and figure sculpture and statues need special authorisation. (An intriguing little exercise is to walk through a churchyard and estimate how many of its memorials would be permitted under today's regulations.)

On materials it couldn't be more explicit:

> All memorials must be made of natural stone with no reflecting finish, or of hardwood. Stones traditionally used in local buildings, or stones closely similar to them in colour and texture, are to be preferred. Black, green, blue or red granite are not permitted ... no black or white marble, synthetic stone or plastic.
>
> *Rules for the Introduction of Churchyard Memorials*

Few, if any, would want to take issue with the preference for local stone. But for the overwhelming majority of monumental

masons and their customers local stone and individual design are
no longer real options. This county cannot produce enough
stone of the durability necessary for memorials; so almost all
stone these days is imported and the few English quarries that
there are, like Dorset, are too far away and do not always
produce stone that would be appropriate in Worcestershire. In
the past there were lots of local quarries to meet local demand
but the cost of quarrying Worcestershire stone would be
prohibitive and now most granite comes from Sweden, most
limestone (harder than English) from Italy and Portugal, and
since the 1950s a number of memorials have been made from
dove-grey Carara marble. Today's mason adds an inscription to
the ready-made stone, chosen from a catalogue by his customer.
Individual touches are usually too expensive.

Natural English stone may last 200 or 300 years, depending
on how far it is affected by frost. But all will have its life
shortened by pollution, even slate — the most longlasting and
workable, the most impervious to weather; and what nature and
pollution don't manage, neglect and vandalism will. Many older
memorials in Worcestershire are of sandstone and, in the south
of the county, Cotswold lime. The latter carves well (and there
are some excellent examples of the mason's work still standing
two centuries and more later), but neither are obvious choices
for monumental work: they are too soft and weather too easily. It
has to be remembered however that the early masons were using
hand tools which could not cut harder stone like granite, and
only with the discovery of tungsten carbide, just over two
centuries ago, could much harder rocks, including granite, be
worked. The result, more or less everywhere, is collapsing
tombs, severed crosses, broken pyramids and headstones that are
crumbling and falling to bits. So much has already gone, those
beyond hope crushed for further use.

Gone with them — or no longer readable, the memorial
surface worn away or covered in lichen or smothered with

brambles and ivy — are thousands upon thousands of epitaphs, rich in information, an invaluable source of local history, but until recently rarely recorded. Epitaphs can reveal for us the everyday lives of a past that really does seem like 'a foreign country': a world of masters and servants, where men — and more particularly women — knew their place, of firm belief and strong superstition; a world where people died younger, children's chances of survival were very much slimmer, where diseases, now tamed, carried off thousands; where death by drowning was common and suicides normally confined to the north part of the churchyard; a world where working for the railway was a source of great pride, where many a teacher held a much-respected place in the community; a world of blacksmiths and wheelwrights and parish clerks who served for ever; and a world where money and status combined to leave us with summaries of lives so perfect we might reach the same conclusion as the American author, Paul Eldridge:

> Reading the epitaphs, our only salvation lies in resurrecting the dead and burying the living.

Or as Dr Samuel Johnson had earlier remarked: 'In lapidary inscriptions a man is not upon oath'. And John Noake positively railed against 'the whole tribe of epitaph writers and eulogists' whose fulsome lines of verse and prose could be read at Besford, Martin Hussingtree, Ribbesford and, he suggested, most other churchyards, constant reminders of the graphic remark that 'if some men could rise again and read their inscriptions, they would fancy they had got into the wrong graves'.

Epitaphs succeed in showing only too well in fact that though the details of daily living may have changed human nature is the same as it ever was — vain and hypocritical, humble and stalwart, murderous and loving, careless and courageous, patient, eccentric and faithful. Many a villain lies buried beneath a great show of a tomb, while many an honest sinner has had nothing to mark his end. Quite what future generations would make of us if our epitaphs were all they had to go on is hard to say, for the art of this particularly specialised form of composition seems almost to have died out. It's partly because of the cost — working stone is very expensive. It's probably also to do with avoiding the long-winded insincerity our forefathers too often indulged in. But they also left us a much richer mix of epitaphs than we are handing on — moving and expressive, tantalising and quirky, informative and specific. Ours by contrast are bland and banal, communicating very little.

In recent years a systematic recording of epitaphs has got under way, prompted by an increased concern about preserving our heritage and by the tremendous interest in family history. Pre-mid-nineteenth century tombstones are being listed by the Historic Buildings and Monuments Commission for England because their superior craftsmanship and originality of design make them of special archaeological and historic interest; and at the same time whole churchyards are being put on fiche by family history societies. In the West Midlands the Birmingham and Midlands Society for Genealogy and Heraldry has been at this task for many years and a lot of work remains to be done; and when examples arise where gravestones, recorded only a few years ago, can no longer be found — or no longer be deciphered — the importance of this volunteer work can be judged.

Epitaphs have been disappearing for a very long time. For his *Collections for the History of Worcestershire,* published in the 1780s, the imperious Treadway Nash noted at Upton-on-Severn the following gem:

> Here lies the body of Mary Ford,
> Whose soul, we hope, is with the Lord:
> But if for hell she's changed this life,
> It's better than being John Ford's wife.

John Ford was apparently a less than perfect husband whose neighbours forced him into accepting this epitaph for his wife. Seventy years later, when Noake looked for it, it had gone. William Cotton describes in his book the exact location of the grave of Thomas Mannaley, a currier who was stabbed to death near Bromsgrove's Town Hall in 1819, somehow dragging himself along St John Street before dying opposite the Shoulder of Mutton. Neither his stone, which told in verse the story of his murder, nor a cross and deep-cut initials carved on a nearby lime tree have been traceable for some years.

And probably the most abbreviated epitaph of all time, from the former parish of St Andrew's, Worcester, was quoted by Thomas Ravenshaw in *Antiente Epitaphes* (1878) but has long gone:

> Short of weight
> H.L.T.B.O.
>   R.W.
> I.H.O.A.J.R.
> A.D.1780.A.63

'R.W.' was Richard Weston, a baker, but it is not clear from Ravenshaw whether the first line was part of the epitaph or from his own pen.

There is an inevitability about all this. Stone memorials will decay, occasionally to the point of becoming dangerous, and churchyards sometimes need more space. In the past this has too often meant standing the stones against the church or perimeter walls (where, unfortunately, they and the walls will decay even faster because of the moisture trapped between them); placing them flat on the grass or using them as paving for the footpaths, thus accelerating the wear to their surfaces; or simply clearing great numbers of them away — to who knows where? A lot of clearing has gone on in Worcestershire — Little Shelsley,

Lining the path like sentries at St Leonard's, Clent

Badsey, Grafton Flyford, Pinvin, Lindridge, Holt, St John in
Bedwardine, Worcester; the list could go on, for all over the
county — and for many years — headstones have been lining
paths like sentries or leaning against walls like unemployed
soldiers. Such exercises have left some of the county's
churchyards bereft of all but a very few memorials — even those
few in some instances herded against the perimeter wall — and
they look rather sad versions of their traditional selves.

The most unusual example of resiting can be seen at Upton-
on-Severn where counters in the heritage and tourist
information centre have been formed from two nineteenth-
century gravestones, one in memory of three members of the
Walker family, John, Jane and their son Charles; the other in
memory of Mary Thomas and her husband Charles, and
William Lowe Ainsworth and his wife Sarah. The old church
and churchyard of St Peter and St Paul were in use until 1879;

but the church was demolished except for the bell tower and some of the gravestones were used to pave the churchyard, a number of these subsequently covered up during alterations to the surrounding area.

A better solution has been the sensitive resiting of stones with family groups kept firmly together. At Cookley, for instance, a number of headstones have been rearranged into several 'henges' and at Pinvin some of the old stones have been cleared away and a group resited to form a standing circle at the edge of the churchyard. But relocation, thoughtful or otherwise, renders quite meaningless that old assertion 'Here lies the body ...'.

The other priceless feature of the churchyard, its natural habitat, is also under attack. On the one hand there is 'the cult of the lawn' as it has been called, the desire to see the churchyard looking like the best of gardens with close-cropped grass, exotic flowers and neat herbaceous borders. ('I'd like to keep the edges a bit wilder for the bees and flowers' said one rueful tender of a churchyard in mid-Worcestershire. 'But what can I do? It's their decision.') In this particular vision long grass, weeds, dandelions and ivy are to be shuddered at — and some gravestones are definitely in the way, obstacles to the easy manoeuvring of the church lawnmower. But churchyards are places where the dead are buried, not private gardens fit for afternoon tea, and it is entirely appropriate that nature should have some say.

It's not new, this desire to domesticate the parish burial ground. Almost a century ago Rev Chafy of Rous Lench, in his short history of the village, wrote in disapproving tone of the former state of the churchyard there, 'as rough and uneven as a turbulent sea'. He was clearly relieved that after some years it was brought to a 'uniform velvet sward', having fallen into 'conscientious hands which never rested till it had attained perfection'. He goes on to quote with obvious pride an article written by Quentin Read of Hampton, near Evesham, a gardening expert, who visited Rous Lench in 1895 and extolled the virtues of the sheer symmetry and perfection of contour of everything that had been planted there — not a hair out of place!

> The walks and grass were kept scrupulously clean and neat, the graves all uniform and of the same height and shape, the grass closely shaven.

Unbridled wilderness on the other hand is not the answer either. There is nothing especially attractive about a churchyard in the grip of cow parsley, stinging nettle, coarse grasses or giant hogweed; and, more to the point, it is not very helpful to the rest of the wildlife there. Somehow there has to be a balance struck between these two extremes if the English churchyard is to retain its character and the flora and fauna are to be given the best chance of survival.

For churchyards are special places, in many country areas the only bits of ancient herb-rich grassland left, home to some wild flowers and grasses rarely seen beyond its boundaries and some wild orchids never found elsewhere. These small plots of earth have been untouched by the changes of the last couple of centuries to the land surrounding them; so in God's Acres, oases of the past, there is an abundance of plant and animal life.

There are, most noticeably, glorious arrays of wild flowers of the meadow, germander, speedwell, sorrel, ox-eye daisies, for instance, many now dependent on churchyards for survival since ploughing and spraying have destroyed over 95% of ancient meadow land in the last three decades; the wild flowers of the woodland, such as red campion, white bryony and stitchwort; and the flowers most of us know best — cowslips, bluebells, daffodils, primroses, snowdrops and many more from the wayside. There are different varieties of grasses, some, like the broad-leaved meadow grass, quite rare; and all the plants that grow on stone, lichens, mosses, ferns and rocky plants, surviving well in the churchyard (though the Midlands region itself has few natural outcrops of rock).

Trees have always been an essential feature of the churchyard's character, none more so than the yew; and the county has many ancient examples. The old form of yew is the spreading tree and there is a fine one for instance at Hampton, near Evesham, another near the south door at Cleeve Prior; and at Abbotts Morton, near the Warwickshire border, a former rector is protected in death by four yew trees which since they were planted over 130 years ago have grown to provide him with a green canopy. The more upright, sometimes topiaried, yew is generally more in evidence. Many other kinds of trees have been planted in our churchyards — oak, beech, elm, cedar and the more exotic monkey-puzzle tree. Perhaps the most striking group of trees are the limes that form a belt around St John's, Bromsgrove. The trees are exactly 200 years old and although a few of their number are missing they still form an impressive sight.

St Michael's, Abberley, cleared and neat, a few stones grouped behind the wall

But there is an awful lot of nature in the churchyard that is on the move — creeping, crawling, hopping, jumping, leaping, running, flying: insects of all descriptions, like butterflies and moths, ladybirds and flies, bugs and beetles and the 'noisy trio', the bees, wasps and grasshoppers. Then there are the birds without whose singing and chattering and squawking no churchyard is complete, nesting and roosting safely in the trees and hedges (or, as at Himbleton, in style above the magnificent door of the church porch), a variety of food at their disposal — blackbirds, chaffinches, housemartins and hedgesparrows, robins and rooks (noisiest of all), swallows, tits, woodpeckers and woodpigeons and the birds of the tower, jackdaws, kestrels and swifts.

Singlehandedly bats could prove how vital conservation in the churchyard is. Originally they were creatures of caves and woodlands but clearance over the centuries has robbed them of their natural habitat and they have had to adapt to living in buildings. Bats in the belfry, yes; and bats in the churchyard, bats in the porch.

The good things in the churchyard also provide food and shelter for a range of mammals — toads and frogs in the damp areas, voles, mice and shrews, squirrels (occasionally red), foxes and badgers. And, of course, rabbits. At Whittington it seemed appropriate that tucked away under the branches of a spreading yew was a headstone in memory of Benjamin Bunn who died in 1816, while under the same tree buxom bunnies played.

It's the easiest thing in the world to advocate the management of a churchyard that will strike just the right balance between nature and memorial. Caring for the churchyard in practice is quite another thing. Even amongst those keenest to preserve what is best there can be conflicting interests. The lichen that prevents the reading and recording of an epitaph may be a specimen of great beauty and interest to the naturalist (and in some instances, where the epitaph has worn away, a source of dating the erection of the memorial). And even where the wisest of plans is drawn up — regularly tending the most frequently used paths and areas, allowing the older areas to flourish as meadow — there is the problem of time, money and, above all, commitment. The signs are that a few Worcestershire parishes are highly organised with rotas of volunteers and a variety of equipment; some pay outsiders to do the best they can in the few hours they have; while others rely on the noble efforts of individuals who have happily looked after churchyards for years and years. But is there anyone to replace that devoted generation?

All over the county there are men who have been looking after things for decades. The highlight of a Spring visit to Bredon's Norton was the long chat with a friendly, humorous 80-year-old. He has been tending the churchyard since he was 25, and for the past 46 years he has been ringing the bells and, twice a week, winding the clock. He was christened there, went to Sunday School there and became the verger. And he still enjoys it. A story he told illustrated only too well the battle between man and nature.

A few years ago someone kept asking him to make sure that when he died he grew some brambles either side of his grave to stop the foxes getting him. He was a younger man than our gardening friend who therefore saw no urgency. But when for the umpteenth time he pestered, 'You won't forget, will you?', our friend decided to answer. 'No, I haven't forgotten. In fact I've started growing them already.' 'You hard b...', the man replied, greatly offended. But the man did die first and, as the gardener laughingly pointed out, the churchyard is far too well kept to let brambles grow — it's all very neat around his grave.

2 Churchyard dramas

 Our ancestors must have known their churchyards pretty well. For hundreds of years they were the focal point of the community: so through the churchyards they walked to attend services on Sundays and holy days and to elect their churchwardens, constables and overseers of the poor; and into the churchyard they rushed to enjoy the village fair, to play games, like cricket and football, to watch mummers and jugglers and wrestling and cockfighting and, sometimes, to get drunk and turn riotous. The authorities attempted to stamp out these secular activities but it wasn't easy, for where there was no village green or town square the churchyard was often the only place for such gatherings. As late as the 1820s Wake Sunday (Trinity Sunday) was the occasion for unruly scenes in the churchyard at Claines — fighting, drunkenness, debauchery; and 'even on the graves, travelling vagabonds plied their profession'.

The fun and games usually took place on the north side of the church for reasons very probably buried in ancient superstition. For it was that side, furthest from the warmth and light of the sun, that was considered to be the most open to attack from the devil; and in the early years of our churchyards it was hard to get anyone to consent to burial there. It only began to fill up when there was no more space in the more favoured areas — the east, chosen by the gentry because closest to the altar, the south, warm and light and 'safe', the west, certainly not desirable but better than the north.

Even when church attendance became less than vigorous and the entertainment had gone from the churchyard the high rate of infant mortality together with a lower life expectancy than ours meant that people's association with God's Acre remained a compelling one. Though we may have been guilty of exaggerating that situation it is still hard for most of us to take in the number of little children's names that are recorded on memorials all over the county.

Five of the children of
JOHN and PHOEBE WOODWARD
CHARLES who died March
1799, Aged 2 Years
HESTER died October
1783, Aged 9 Months
ELIZABETH did August
1789, Aged 3 Years
DANIEL, died August
1796, Aged 6 Years
JOSEPH, died August
1796, Aged 2 Years.

(St John the Baptist, Wolverley)

The opening formality of every burial took place at the lychgate whose purpose was to provide shelter for the coffin and its bearers (from the Old English word *lic*, meaning corpse). Here they waited at the edge of consecrated ground until the officiating minister arrived to conduct the funeral, the coffin meanwhile resting on a stone or wooden ledge. A great many of

Free to the parish: the bier at St Eadburgha's, Broadway

our lychgates have been rebuilt during the last 100 years and from some of the older ones these ledges have been removed to allow for more comfortable access. But in the days when there were no cars to drive right up to the porch door they were a vital little detail.

The bearers too may have needed a rest for if the deceased had been poor they would have had some carrying to do. They might have been luckier, though, for some parishes had wheeled biers available to the poor free of charge. There is a wonderful bier with stretcher in St Eadburgha's, Broadway, given in 1888 in memory of Rev Caffin, vicar for 25 years, for the free use of all parishioners. There were always those, of course, who were too poor to have a coffin: some were carried to the grave in the parish coffin, their bodies removed and lowered into the ground; the poorest of all were lowered into a large hole that was covered over only when filled up.

For what happened on consecrated ground was largely

determined by social standing. Though they might avoid a pauper's grave many a poor soul would leave this earth with no stone to mark their remains — their only memorial the churchyard cross, in early Anglo-Saxon times the outstanding Christian symbol, often pre-dating the church. In the thirteenth century the Bishop of Worcester ordered a cross to be erected in every churchyard in the diocese; and the cross was still the predominant feature in the churchyard 300 years later. But civil strife and general anti-papism in the seventeenth and eighteenth centuries left most of them in a very damaged state and in later years heads and shafts were added to the ancient bases, often inappropriate in design.

Few of the earliest crosses survived because most were made of wood; and the fragments that have been found have been moved inside churches and museums. Rare too are complete medieval crosses standing in their original location; but there are a number in various degrees of incompleteness throughout the

The remains of a fourteenth-century cross at Pirton

county, like the one at St Kenelm's, Clifton-upon-Teme, which
is a modern cross on a medieval base; and the stumpy remains of
a fourteenth-century cross at Pirton.

A slight step up from no memorial at all was the simple metal
gravemarker, dwarfed by surrounding headstones and simply
rammed into the soil. There are a few of these in
Worcestershire, the most memorable a cluster, from the second
half of the last century, at Madresfield which record the barest
details of the deaths of James and Ellen Corle, their six children
(none surviving beyond six years of age) and Grandma Corle
who lived to 80. In the south of the same churchyard there are
two more iron gravemarkers — encircled crosses on a V-shaped
shaft — to brothers who both died in 1879, Archie Weaver aged
14 and Alfred aged 10.

The best chance the poor had of attaining gravestone status
was as servants to others; in return for decades of devotion a
better-off employer would register his or her thanks in stone (see
chapter 4); and occasionally there were other workers in the
village whose stone was paid for by genuinely appreciative
neighbours. Could this have been the case at Little Comberton
where there is a simple headstone to William Copstone who died
25 January 1850, aged 50, 'for many years a respected labourer
of this parish'?

The act of burial itself has been the stuff of numerous
unseemly and bizarre stories, the frankly fictional and the 'real
life' accounts which started out somewhere near the truth but
have been subject to a few added drops of local colour: stories of
inadequate gravedigging (confirmed by Thomas Turner,
eighteenth-century Sussex shopkeeper, schoolmaster and
undertaker, who recorded in his diary that the body of Alice
Stevens, 28-year-old spinster, having been carried two miles by
the bearers, had to be laid on the ground for a time while the
hole was made a bit larger); of people falling into open graves at
night (distinctly possible); of sextons, bearers, even parsons,

The metal gravemarkers of the Corle family at Madresfield

arriving at the graveside drunk; of dramatic churchyard quarrels between grieving relatives and Anglican incumbents.

Worcestershire has had its fair share of such incidents, reminders that churchyards are not always acres of peace and brotherly love. From the parish registers of St John in Bedwardine, Worcester, for instance, comes the story of a bitter dispute between an unbending minister and a strong- minded woman. On 2 August 1741 John Web was buried in his wife's grave 'in my freehold, my church' records the vicar. A few weeks later Web's sister decided to put a large headstone on his grave. With stone and stonecutter in tow she arrived at the churchyard, demanding the key from the clerk. The vicar, incensed that his prior approval had not been sought, ordered the stonecutter away and for her 'insolence' refused Web's sister the necessary permission — unless, he added, she paid 40/−, a steep price at the time. Web's sister offered, after a while and

through a third party, a guinea; the vicar refused and the
bargaining continued. It was the vicar in the end who agreed to
accept 25/– 'for peace sake' — not that the lady handed it over
in person: she got the surveyor of highways to do that. But
exactly three months after his death John Web's stone was
erected.

155 years later to the day, and half-a-dozen miles to the north,
a man called William Hartland was buried at St Mary de
Witton's in Droitwich. There was nothing out of the ordinary
about Hartland but the minister, Rev John Williamson, Rector
of St Andrew's, was noticeably drunk; and the incident was one
of a long list of offences — mostly relating to drunkenness in
public — read out before the Bishop of Worcester at the
Consistory Court in the Chapter House. The complaint against
the rector was made by two men from well-known Droitwich
families, Harry Shirley Jones (buried at St Peter de Witton's in
1917) and Edward Holt Onions (buried at St Mary's eight years
after Hartland). The hearing received national attention, with
headlines like 'Clerical Scandal at Droitwich', because
Williamson's was the first case to be heard under the new Clergy
Discipline Act. He was defrocked and deprived of all his
ecclesiastical positions.

Those who could afford it — and they increased in number as
wealth spread downwards in the seventeenth and eighteenth
centuries — next turned their attention to the memorial, either a
new one to be shaped and carved and lettered or an existing one
on which to have an inscription added. Most people would have
to settle for a headstone, the most popular memorial of all, short
and stubby at first, large and thick as the years passed, slimming
down towards the end of the eighteenth century and decreasing
in size as it took on the medieval-window shapes the Victorians
so admired. The headstone would normally be worked on one
side with a sunken panel to take the inscription, a border and
perhaps some symbolic sculpture. In the seventeenth century

the most popular graveyard symbol was the skull and crossbones. Examples of these, though usually very worn, still tend to shock the twentieth-century eye; but it is worth remembering that stone images of hollow-eyed grinning skulls, of brooding death's-heads, of the scythes of the 'Grim Reaper', the hourglass and the reclining skeleton reflect the attitude towards death of a particular religious philosophy which saw only trials and tribulations in this life, which felt the need to remember man's mortality at all times and expected happiness and fulfilment only from beyond the grave. The symbols of this expectation, fig and pomegranate for prosperity, rope for eternity, the anchor for hope and the rising sun denoting the soul's resurrection, can be seen in a number of Worcestershire churchyards.

When puritan sternness had abated in the eighteenth century winged cherubs and angels became popular and when, a little later, the classical revival got under way urns and a variety of

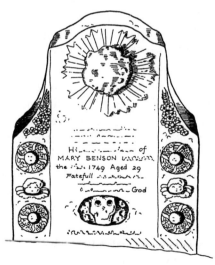

The dramatic headstone to Mary Benson, Bromsgrove: sun, skull and cherubs

other delicate architectural motifs were carved on all manner of memorials. In country areas fruit and flowers and stooks of corn were particularly popular and, more interesting to the local historian, masons found themselves being asked to carve the occupational tools and equipment of the deceased.

And what should be said of the dead? Early gravestones in keeping with the spirit of the age stuck to basic facts: name, age and date of 'departure'. 'Here lyeth the body of ...' was the usual way of recording the event, sometimes less poetically, 'Mary Smith was buried here'. But even in the seventeenth century personal touches were creeping in as a Broadway tomb shows:

> Here lye the Bodies of William Dickin & Mary his Wife who lived
> Comfortably together in this Parish sixty -- years and had thirteen
> (children)

Perhaps the Dickins are early examples of the desire that grew to say more about the deceased: the cause of his death, the way illness is borne, and increasingly his occupation. At the same time verses began to appear confirming the dead person's confidence in a resurrected life, extolling his virtues and expressing his family's sorrow. There is an excellent example of resurrection verse at Church Lench where 'ẙ Body of Marris Hiatt of Abberton', together with his wife's, lies buried. He was 84 when he died in 1714 and the gravestone, now laid flat, shows a characteristic absence of all punctuation and a problem with layout:

> Since thought may doubt whether dry bones may live
> Faith doth answer to the Scruple give
> It sayes they may nay more it sayes they must
> Ye dishonoured bodyes of the Iust
> Shall rise in glory even out of dust

In Harvington, near Evesham, there are two very moving epitaphs from the first half of the eighteenth century. The first records the deaths of four children of Nicholas and Sarah Marshall who died between 1711 and 1721. Their double headstone has four little faces worked in relief across the top and a simple verse follows the details of death:

Here Lies the Bodies of Four Children Dear
Which cause Their Parents to shead Many a tear

Nearby is a very well preserved but sunken headstone to 'Elizabeth the wife of Richard Smith', who died 20 November 1733 aged 36. Only one line of the verse remains readable:

Go home my frendes and Cese from tears

But throughout the eighteenth century the loss of small children was often still being recorded with little or no

The Marshall children, Harvington, near Evesham

comment. A simple headstone at Bromsgrove relates the bare details of the death of three children of John and Sarah Hunt — William in 1736 aged three years and seven months, Hannah in 1738 who hadn't quite reached three, and Joseph in 1742, a tiny baby of five weeks. Seven years later John himself died though his wife lived for another seventeen years. Sometimes though an accompanying verse says something of the stoicism that parents felt they should present to the world. A little headstone at Severn Stoke, most of its lettering in excellent condition, reads:

HERE LYETH THE BODY OF MARGARET,
THE DAUGHTER OF WILLIAM & MARGARET
THORNELOE.
WHO DIED JUNE 2ND 1715 IN THE
5TH YEAR OF HER AGE.
Let Parents strive to be Content
All comes from GOD Is only Lent.
In Youth & Childwood put no trust
For (all) (m)ust Die and come to Dust.

(It *is* Childwood and not Childhood)

Variations of this verse were probably widespread. Thirty years earlier a similar verse was used when one-year-old Elienor Coale was buried at Little Comberton — her headstone could be seen until recent clearing; and before it became unreadable there was a two-line verse on the headstone of Mary Fownes, another one-year-old who was buried at Bromsgrove in 1721:

I but began to live that I might die
And only dyd to live eternally

Probably the most common verse was the one which reminded the living that their time would come. While it is easy to see that Christians who believe in a better life beyond the grave may want to remind those left behind of the joys in store, it is hard to come to terms with the rather threatening and gloating terms in which these reminders of death were so often couched, even where children and young people were involved:

> Art thou in Health and Spirit gay
> I too was so the other day.
> And thought myself of Life as Safe
> As thou who reads't my Epitaph

This was to commemorate the death of Catherine Stew who died in 1802 aged 20 and is buried at Bredon. When John Cole died in 1858 at Sedgeberrow his parents had the following gloomy lines carved on their 10-year-old son's headstone:

> How numerous are the mouldering dead
> How fast man's lives decline;
> Soon may thy tombstone here be read,
> Who now are reading mine.

And when Francis Ballard, South Littleton's stonemason, died in 1811 it seems odd to us that the verse addressed to his wife and children should end with the comfortless assertion that 'death the strongest bands will part'.

Warnings from the grave were still acceptable towards the end of the last century as the headstone of William Raybould, mine host at the Golden Cross Inn, Friar Street, Droitwich, makes clear. Two lines are addressed to its 'Readers':

> What faults you have seen in me, take care to shun
> Look at home, there is plenty to be done.
>
> (St Nicholas, Droitwich)

A memorial to Esther and Thomas Poyner that must have been quite old fashioned when erected at Grimley in the 1860s — a plain double headstone (though much smaller than its

eighteenth-century predecessors) — also has a warning verse that
had been going out of fashion:

> Weep not for me
> For as I am
> Soon thou must be
> Therefore prepare
> To follow me.

But the need to cut the living down to size had largely passed
and a gentler and more personal approach to loss became
evident. Just off the A38 in Barbourne, Worcester, is the small
churchyard of St George with St Mary Magdalene, its
remaining headstones propped against the wall, still in good
condition and handsomely inscribed. One of these is to Mary,
daughter of George and Ann Williams, who died in 1846 when
she was fifteen.

> Sweet maid! from
> Griefs and dangers
> Rest here for ever free;
> We leave thy Dust
> With strangers.
> But oh! we leave not thee.

William Herbert Walsh, who died in 1851 before he reached his
first birthday, is described on his headstone at Little Comberton
as a 'flower which God hath transplanted into his garden'. The
most moving of all memorials to children in the county stands in
the pretty churchyard of St Michael, Little Witley, where a little
headstone in fond memory of four-year-old Claire Egger who
died in 1914 reads:

> Is it well with the child
> It is well

Who wrote these earlier verses, though? The great and wealthy would often have the services of the country's leading poets. The overwhelming majority of lesser mortals would have to make do with the parson, sometimes the schoolmaster, occasionally the squire, the most educated trio in the parish. They would advise the mason on spelling and punctuation and suggest suitable phrasing, 'borrowing' perhaps from poets, concocting slightly different versions; and increasingly the parson would take to composing his own full-blown verses. The result was usually something between the homely and excruciating including the trite, the sickly and the vain.

Very occasionally we get to know precisely who wrote a particular epitaph. In St Andrew's churchyard at Hampton, near Evesham, is a very handsome chest tomb to John Martin who died in 1714. Affixed to one side is a slate panel, its incised letters painted gold (presumably replacing an earlier stone inset)

The splendid tomb of John Martin, Hampton, the epitaph written by his son

and offering the reader the following full-blooded verse:

> Beyond ye prophets settled term
> > of age
> Wither'd & dry I then dropt
> > off ye stage
> And here amidst my kindred clods
> > do lye
> Till time dissolve into eternity
> And sacred angels heav'ly
> > Trumpets sound
> Shall make ye earth its num'rous
> > Dead resound
> Then all my scatter'd ashes shall
> > Revive
> And changed mortality forever live.
> > Vivit post funera victor

It was written by his pious and industrious son who died twenty years earlier at the age of seventeen and whose headstone stands next to his father's memorial.

In Crowle churchyard there is a headstone to John Day Holbeche who died in 1824 aged 31. It's largely a standard version of warning but it unsuccessfully changes rhythm half way through and, without drawing breath, moves straight into an unusually concentrated and non-rhyming version of the period's most mechanical description of a deceased male:

> Reader Stand here and shed a tear
> Over this earth of mine
> For little do you know how soon
> the same fate may be thine
> In bloom of life I was cut down
> Death little warning gave

Let none suppose they can repent too soon
I found it night before I thought it noon
A loving Husband a tender Father
A faithful Friend a good neighbour

A more regular version of these last two lines can be seen, amongst other places, on a tomb in St Andrew's churchyard, Ombersley.

The corresponding set piece to a woman is similarly widespread, lording her virtues as tender wife, dear mother and good friend. Sarah Jones who died in 1844 and lies in Kempsey churchyard is so summed up; and so (though at much greater length) is Ann Proctor who was buried at Ashton-under-Hill in 1797. A particularly contorted example was already difficult to read in St John's, Bromsgrove, over 100 years ago but was well worth recording:

Pale death will hardly find a Nother:-
So Good a wife so kind a Mother
In all her actions so discreet
Was She who here lies at your feet.

The Thrupps' memorial at Shrawley, Joseph who died in 1860 and Frances who died three years later, shows both these two favourite kinds of epitaphs of the day.

Standardised epitaphs came with industrialisation and the much quicker spread of ideas and fashions; and in the nineteenth century a small band of professionals were writing and syndicating their verses to be used for all kinds of endings. One of the most frequently seen deals with the death that comes after a long illness — and it doesn't say a lot for the medical profession of the day. An excellent example exists at Claines on a very large headstone affixed to the outside of the church's north wall. Thomas Hartwright died in 1771, outliving his wife Mary by eighteen years. But his end was probably painful:

> Afflictions sore long time I bore
> Phisicitians were in vain,
> Till Death did Seaze, and God was pleased
> To Ease me of my Pain.

Some original ones continued to get through of course like the rare memorial at Tibberton:

> Sarah, Mother-in-law of
>   Edward Houghton
> Died Jan. 18 1837 aged 84 yrs.

and in the intriguingly bitter little verse on the gravestone of Ann Turner who died in 1836 and is buried in Powick churchyard:

> Do not believe every man's repose,
> For sceming friends prove often the greatest foes
> In fairest meadows dangerous adders lie
> And most deceit is clad in flattery
> Which in deluding counsellors is shown
> Not for thy gain or profit but their own.

Who wrote this particular warning from the grave? It has a distinctly personalised feel about it. But not the mason, presumably.

Some of the best, sadly, have long disappeared, readable only where recorded by others, like the pithy epitaph on the tomb of Richard Wilkes who was buried at Bromsgrove in 1811, aged 80:

> Here lies the just and truly honest man
> Say more I dare not and say less who can.

and the verse on the grave of John Smith of Dodford (also at Bromsgrove) who died in July 1729, exactly six months after his wife Elizabeth:

> Death a short space did Man and Wife divide
> To live without her he a little tried
> Found it to hard a task and then he died
> In all Relations They Behaved so Well
> You'l scarcely Match Them with a Parallel.

The greatest temptation for grieving friends and relatives, however, must have been to settle for nothing less than perfection. There's an old Gaelic saying: 'Die, if you want to be praised' and there are numerous examples in Worcestershire, as in other counties, of summaries of lives impossibly good. John Tovey, for instance, who died in 1841 and is buried in a tomb under an old spreading yew tree at the east side of the church at Church Lench, was probably a very good chap. But was he really this good?

> A man of distinguished Talents — of great Attainments and of exemplary Piety With him Science was the Handmaid of Religion and made subservient to its Interest.

John Noake got regularly worked up about this 150 years ago. At Martin Hussingtree it was a gentleman by the name of Ruffhead who set him off — or, rather, his 'doting relict' whose husband's accomplishments she had chosen permanently (more or less) to parade in stone 'before the few rustics who weekly tread the floor of that little sanctuary'. In Ribbesford he found the epitaphs laudatory to the point of nauseam, reminding him of the story of the little girl who visited the cemetery of Père la Chaise in Paris and after reading the fulsome praises on one tomb after another wanted to know where all the sinners were buried.

What then did Noake make of the epitaph on the tomb of
Joseph Chillingworth who was buried at Tardebigge in 1788?

> His Life throughout, He labour'd to Improve
> In trade, in Virtue, and in social (?Law)
> His heart was good religiously inclin'd
> His temper sweet Benevolent and kind
> His manner open, Generous and free.
> He was a man, Such as a man should (be).
> This truth he prov'd in every path H(e trod)
> An honest Man's, the noblest work of (God)
> A Single life he led, on wisdom's plan:
> Go imitate the Virtues of the Man.

Apart from the observation that the curious mid-line
punctuation would suggest the eulogy originally was meant to
be set out as twenty, not ten, lines, he would no doubt have

The fulsome epitaph to Joseph Chillingworth at Tardebigge

repeated the conclusion he drew on his Martin Hussingtree visit that it would seem 'our churches were raised rather for the lording of men than for the praise and glory of God'.

Epitaphs, of course, have always been a problem. Who is prepared to write ill — even truthfully — of the dead?

Friend! for your epitaphs I'm grieved,
Where still so much is said,
One half will never be believed,
The other never read.

This was from that sophisticated poet and satirist Alexander Pope, written over 200 years ago. But Worcestershire has made its own contribution to this school of thought in the form of a poem which can be ready in the country's only church dedicated to St Barbara at Ashton-under-Hill:

Reader what Needes a panegurick skill,
A limmers pensill or a poets quill
They are but miserable comforters
When badd ones die that paint their sepulchers
and when the life in holiness is spent
the naked -- a marble monument
To keepe from rotting piety and alarmes
Doe farr excell the best aegyptian balmes
Then whosoever thou art the course is safe
Live like thy selfe both toombe and epitaph.

> Amori Ergo Posuit
> April 8 Ano Dom 1651

Something more truthful occasionally got through (in the earlier centuries, anyway), like Mary Ford's at Upton-on-Severn (see page 22); and the inscription on a headstone to John Guley Senr. at Cofton Hackett, 'in expectation of the last Day. What sort of man he was, that Day will discover ...'. In fact, though, he was one of a stalwart band of voluntary workers, parish clerk for 55 years, and this rather dubious-sounding epitaph can be found in a few other churchyards.

Nearly all epitaphs, it has to be remembered, reflect to a large extent the beliefs and fashions of their time. Few people in a state of grief are able to resist the advice of the 'experts' and this must have been doubly so at a time when very few of our ancestors could read or write. Lacking the confidence which comes with education, they must have been putty in the parson's hands; and we may have to consider that the menacing verses from the grave or the apparently calm acceptance of the death of a child say much more about the views of the Christian church than the individual mourners.

For local and family historians, of course, it's the detailed information about individual lives of the past which makes epitaphs so important a source. One of the county's very best examples is a well preserved and beautifully-lettered headstone to the Lilley family which stands very near to the south entrance of St John's, Bromsgrove:

> To the Memory of Three children of Stephen and Sarah Lilley. and Grand Children to Richard and Mary Harbert. Interr'd Underneath this Stone Elizabeth their Daughter Departed this Life August the 25th 1747 Aged 5 Years. Also Ann their Daughter Departed this Life February the 16th 1748 Aged 2 Hours. Also Sarah their Daughter Departed this Life August the 31st 1761 Aged 23 Years.
> Mourn not for us our Parents Dear.
> Wait but a while you'l soon be here.
> Also to the Memory of Sarah the Wife of Stephen Lilley and Grand Daughter to the aforesaid Alderman Harbert and the late Alderman Tilt; She Departed this Life June the 15th 1775 Aged 70 Years.

Apart from the shortest life to be recorded in a Worcestershire churchyard, family historians will smack their lips at the

The Lilley family's headstone at St John's, Bromsgrove

detailed relationships of three generations, note the late child-bearing of Mrs Lilley and then have to sort out the mason's mistake in the latter part of the inscription. And where is Stephen Lilley? It could well be him resting in Tibberton churchyard.

Not everybody died young as churchyards can confirm. People are often surprised by the sheer numbers who have lived to an advanced age. Across the churchyard from two-hour-old Ann Lilley lies Dorothy Lowis who was 100 when she died in 1827; at St Michael's, Abberley, the churchyard was cleared in 1963 but a few headstones were integrated into a small walled space beyond the west end of the old chapel, including one to Mary Bagnall who died in 1836 at 102; in Stoulton there is a gravestone to William Palfrey who died in 1894, also aged 102; yet another 102 year-old, William Walker, was buried at Hanley Castle a year later; and the oldest recorded person of all, Mary

Lane, lies buried at Childswickham. Her modest headstone
which now lies flat in the grass is interesting to say the least:

> MARY LANE
>   BAPT
> MARCH 15 1618
>   DIED
> OCT 15 1741
> AGED 133 YEARS

Did someone have difficulty adding up? Or was she ten years old
when she was baptised? It was not unusual for baptisms to take
place when the baby had become a toddler or even a small child;
but ten seems a shade on the late side.

Establishing an ancestor's age at the time of death can often be
a problem for the genealogist. Yet it is not surprising that a
certain vagueness should have crept into some gravestones
during a time when it was the baptism rather than the birth that
was registered and when it seemed to matter less to the average
man that he should know the date of his birth. We are told, for
instance, that John Wood of Caunsell, Wolverley, was 'about 30
years' when he died in 1684; and over half a century later Ann
Ryland, buried at Tibberton, is 'Aged 31 and upwards'.
Presumably someone at least knew when she had been baptised.

Gravestones can also tell us something about the kinds of
illnesses and diseases that once killed so many. Exactly 150 years
ago 'Emily and Fanny the affectionate children of George &
Fanny Oldaker ... died of scarlet fever after a few days illness'.
They were fifteen and twelve years of age and were buried in the
churchyard at Cropthorne. At Mamble, among a number of
gravestones to the Mapp family, is one to Eliza Mapp who died
of consumption in 1877. As a reminder that fever was no
respecter of persons, and that in particular cholera was not
confined to the poorest and most insanitary part of towns, there

is a tomb to Eliza Susanna Jacob, mother of the headmaster of Bromsgrove School. She was one of eighteen people who died during the cholera visitation of 1832 and is buried in the small area in the north-west of St John's churchyard that was put aside for the victims.

One noticeable feature of churchyards is the number of gravestones to those who died not from illness but from accidental drowning. It should not take us too much by surprise if we remember that before seaside holidays got under way — and for a long time after that if you were poor — learning to swim simply did not arise. A look at the Worcester papers during the eighteenth and nineteenth centuries reveals that two or three people were drowned most weeks. Predictably, they were often young and male, the adventurous element in society, like Thomas Smithin, 14-year-old son of the village blacksmith at Birlingham, who was drowned at Ashton Pirton Pool in 1746. The verse on his headstone makes it clear that a 'spectator' tried to save him. It was February, so perhaps he had been skating on the ice like Joseph and John Bourne who were drowned while skating in Westwood Park in 1865. It was July 1876 when Charles Baylis of Pinvin was accidentally drowned. He was 19 and had been bathing. It was also in July, 21 years later, that William Charles West was drowned. His death, unlike the others, made the 'Latest News' column of *Berrow's Worcester Journal*. He was 13 years of age and had been staying with his aunt for a few days when he went off to Hallow Ford with a group of boys, tried to cross the river but, realising he could not make it, turned back. He was only 10 or 12 yards from the bank when he drowned.

It is the symbol of death in battle, however, that most often strikes the churchyard visitor, the plain white stones that mushroomed overnight to remind us of the endless thousands of young men who died in the First World War, often far from home.

In addition to information, we can discover in our churchyards a lot about the ideas and fashions and attitudes of former ages, from what gravestones *don't* say as much as what they do. Apart from the odd publican and servants with appreciative employers, where are the gravestones which record the work done by women in previous centuries, for example? Either they confined themselves to the duties of wife, mother and good neighbour, or the day-to-day work they did was not thought worthy of mention. Where are the female parish clerks and overseers and organists and sextons? We know very well they did not exist and it is well on into the nineteenth century before we get the first village schoolmistresses commemorated.

Just as telling as these gaps is the way in which women were for so long defined in terms of their husband or father. In Salwarpe churchyard Williamina Mary Byam Martin, who died in 1895 aged 75, is described merely as the youngest daughter of Admiral of the Fleet Sir T Byam Martin; in Bromsgrove the gravestone of Dorothy Lowis, mentioned above, gives much more detail about her father and grandfather, the latter as Governor of Londonderry, commanding the forces which were attacked by James II's army after the battle of the Boyne. In Kempsey there is a memorial to Samuel Webb, 'for twenty-four years the much respected Landlord of the Crown Inn in this Parish'. When his wife died later in the same year, 1871, she was simply 'wife of the above'; and at Malvern Priory, tucked away amongst the trees, is a memorial to Lydia Plumptree which says nothing about her but quite a bit about her father (a former President of Queen's College, Cambridge, prebendary of Norwich Cathedral) whose last surviving daughter she was. Between them these four women were on this earth for 335 years; three of them were almost certainly well educated; the fourth was almost certainly a crucial part of the family business.

Whatever the epitaph decided upon by the grieving family there was an immediate problem to be faced as soon as the burial was finished: how to stave off a possible attempt at robbery. Up until 1832 the medical profession had to rely upon the executed bodies of criminals for the purpose of research. These were nowhere near enough; so a scandalous trade grew up between, on the one hand, the bodysnatchers — or resurrection men — who operated so swiftly they could dig up a newly buried body and offer it to a hospital like Worcester Infirmary, or Oxford, or even one of the teaching hospitals in London, within 24 hours of burial; and, on the other hand, unscrupulous surgeons who were prepared to pay up to £20 for the corpses and ask no questions. Sometimes watch huts were erected in churchyards to deter the grave-robbers; those who could afford it had railings immediately put around their graves or massively heavy slabs laid on top of the newly dug soil (which unfortunately inhibited decomposition); and those who could rise to neither of these made use of the parish slab for a few days until the body ceased to be fresh enough for anatomical purposes.

Reports of particularly gruesome examples of bodysnatching can be read in Worcestershire newspapers up to the very eve of new legislation — at Hanley Castle in January 1831, at Broadway in the following month; and on 24 November of that same year Joseph Rose, sexton in Bromsgrove for nearly 45 years, wrote in his notebook that three bodies had been stolen, presumably during the night. The robbers, sometimes operating in groups, grew quite sophisticated and often seem to have gone undetected; perhaps not surprisingly in an age of poor, if any, lighting and no real police force. In 1832, however, an Act of Parliament put an end to bodysnatching almost overnight by making available to the medical profession bodies from additional sources such as workhouses.

Joseph Rose must have been as relieved as all the other sextons in the county. But his family would have seen it all, for his father, grandfather and brother had already served as sextons and clerks and after his death in 1869 his son, who fell to his death from the belfry, and then his great nephew were to do the same. The duties of the sexton were wideranging: winding the clock, keeping the church and churchyard clean, ringing the bells (every night, usually, and three times on Sundays) and having eyes in the back of his head, for it wasn't just bodies that were stolen — sundials were levered off walls, brass plaques, leaded into the stonework of tombs, were removed.

But there have always been people who have worried about what would happen to their bodies or bones after they died. At the foot of the headstone to the Beach family against the south wall of the church at Shrawley is a horizontal slab with a metal rectangle on which is inscribed:

> It is requested by John Beach that this stone be not
> removed 1850

Not until the mason finally put the stone in place did his customer know quite what he was getting. For especially in the earlier years there were many gaps between the theory of the parson and schoolmaster and the practical skill of the craftsman. The lettering was often very primitive, almost childlike; but the really striking thing is how varied it was. A walk through St John's, Bromsgrove, for instance, or Ribbesford, near Bewdley, reveals how different both in skill and style one seventeenth-century gravestone can be from the next. Some stones have firm letters deeply incised, others do little more than scratch the surface; some have only capital letters, not always straight and often badly spaced, with words, including names, abbreviated or carved above another or split and carried over to the next line or into the border around the inscription panel, all signs of the mason's miscalculation of the line's length. Near the east end of the church at St John's, Bromsgrove, is a double headstone recording the deaths of the Kimberley family over a period of almost 100 years and a typical example of a rather unsophisticated approach to inscriptions:

Here lyeth the Body of Rob
ert Kimberley he departed
this life ye 31 1659
Also Elizabeth his wife dep
arted this life Nov ye 16 1688
Also William Kimberley dep
arted this life Nov ye 8 1680
Also here lyeth the Body of
Robert Kimberley of Shepley
late Alderman of ye Parish of
Bromsgrove he departed this
life April ye 22 1757 aged 71

Above,

Doat not on Earthly things, Seek joys
In Blissful Mansions of Eternal Love.

Punctuation was often non-existent; and spelling, even allowing
for the general inconsistency of the time, 'individual':

Here lyeth the body of
John Wood Juneor of
Caunsall who deseased
May the 16th 1684
Aged about 30 years

(St John the Baptist, Wolverley)

Perhaps 'diseased' reflects the way the word was pronounced.
   But other headstones of the same period show a much more
skilful use of upper-and-lower-case letters and some display real
style. There seems to be no golden rule about the later work
being automatically better: all depended on the ability of the
local mason at the time.

'Trooman' Richard Clark, buried at Ribbesford

All over the county there are heartwarming examples of man's little imperfections. At Ribbesford there is a headstone to a 'Trooman' of Bewdley (Trowman or Freeman?) and at Longdon John Beale is recorded as having died in 1873 at Lake Charles, Louisiana, in *South* America (but perhaps we should blame the family or consulted 'experts' for that). At Chaddesley Corbett the mason made a classic error which many of us make on the first day of each new year. On a slab close to the end of the church he carved:

Here Lyeth $\overset{e}{y}$ Body of $\overset{r}{m}$ John Newman who departed this life 26th day of March 170$\frac{6}{7}$.

It is necessary to remember that at this point in our history there were in a sense two starts to the year, 1 January and 25 March, the feast of the Annunciation of the Virgin Mary, the first of the quarter days and start of the Christian calendar. So the year in the period from 1 January to 24 March was regularly shown with five figures — 1694/5, 1703/4, for example. From 25 March to the end of the year it was written as we would write it. Clearly, the mason had forgotten about the 'new' year. But the interesting question is: was this joined form his own particular style or, having wrongly committed himself to the figure '6', did he try to put things right by carving over it?

For most of its history the churchyard was a deeply familiar place to its parishioners, and as they went to and fro the names on the headstones they passed would have been almost entirely local — the Bomfords at Atch Lench Baptist chapel, Marshall Halls and Ashwins at Bretforton, Crumps at Hampton, Dowdeswells at Bushley, Toveys at Church Lench, Amphletts at Bromsgrove and Wychbold and Ombersley, Onions in Droitwich, Worralls at Ribbesford, Tandys and Curnocks at Rous Lench, the Yeends at Rous Lench and Little Comberton, Holyoakes at Tardebigge, the Callows and Freemans and Thorniloes at Grimley, and spreading across a number of parishes the Bournes and Bullocks, Corbetts and Harbers, the Thrupps and the Jelfs. In many Worcestershire churchyards the family thread remains unbroken but in the last 100 years or so new names have appeared of people born further and further away, especially in places like Malvern and Kemerton whose gravestones reflect their status as fashionable areas for retirement.

3 The end of a working day

Gravestones are something of a paradox. Unique productions, in that they record the burial of particular individuals, they nevertheless verge so often on the anonymous, telling us next to nothing about the named. In a sense they may be said to be at best aids to creative speculation, at worst departure points for flights of fancy. The reader is almost always left wondering what the deceased looked like: not for an English churchyard the European practice of including pictures of the dead — though a rather macabre exception exists among the very few stones left in St John in Bedwardine, Worcester, and there are a number now in Worcestershire cemeteries. Even the gravestone of Robert Reeve, 'the Ripple Giant' who died in 1626 and is said to have stood over seven foot tall, seems to give little away. But perhaps 350 years ago when the churchyard was much less cluttered the two-line verse was more telling for the distance between his head- and footstone would have been obvious:

As you passe by behold my length,

But never glory in your Strength

There are however quite a lot of surviving memorials which tell us something about the kind of work our ancestors did. Most do so by means of a brief factual statement, quite often followed by a verse penned by one of the local intelligentsia or taken from a printed collection of lines deemed appropriate. A few — a very few, in fact — provide us with pictures in stone of the tools, equipment, even the setting of occupations pursued normally right up to death. At Broadway, for instance, the headstone of William Hasland, who died in 1786, displays the scissors, comb, razor and quill you would expect a village barber to have used. The headstone to a gamekeeper at Shrawley which stands — or rather leans — just to the west of the church porch was until comparatively recently a splendid example: above the bare details recording Thomas Cooke's death in 1814 is a sculptured scene in an oval inset, a gamekeeper, with his dog, in the act of shooting at two birds; and below a verse, slight variations of which are found in other parts of the country:

He sleeps. No more at early Morn
To wake the wood with Mellow Horn
No more with willing Dog and Gun
To rise before the Sluggard sun
No more beside the Social can
Tomorrow's sport with joy to plan
Death took his aim, discharg'd his piece
And bade his sporting season cease.

Sadly, part of the picture has worn and most of the epitaph is impossible to read, so that we must now rely on earlier written records.

Most of the inscription has also worn on Richard Jones' gravestone which just catches the shade of a large tree in the

Richard Jones, canal builder at Finstall

long burial ground at Finstall running between the road and the railway line. But the oval inset at the top of the stone shows very clearly in relief the tools of a man involved in the building of the nearby Worcester—Birmingham Canal — compass, set square, trowel, spade, ladder and what look like a ruler and possibly a lock gate. Jones was 46 when he died and the stone was erected by his fellow workmen at the canal company; that much is still readable. But a lot more of Richard Jones' story emerges from newspaper accounts of his death. He was, it seems, a bricklayer, living with his wife and six children in a cottage at Bitford Lock, Claines. On the night of 23 April 1840 he decided to take a rest in the middle of the Droitwich road (just, significantly, near the Crown Inn) when he was run over by the Bristol to Birmingham Mail. The puzzling thing is why he was buried in Finstall and not at Claines.

Another fatal accident gave rise to an unusual stone in Hanbury where Henry Parry, not yet 21, was buried in 1847.

The death of Henry Parry, depicted on his headstone at Hanbury

What are we to make of the scene depicted in bas relief — a railway with a horse and truck on it and a young man who seems to be tumbling across the rails? According to John Noake, the young man was a 'railway labourer' who was knocked down either by the horse or the truck.

Two of the most famous memorials in the country stand side by side in Bromsgrove churchyard. Painted black and white, their appearance is striking; and regularly reproduced in books on railway history their stories are so familiar. Yes, Scaife and Rutherford, driver and fireman, killed when their engine blew up. That must be it on Rutherford's stone, the Norris. But the headstones, to say the least, are misleading. Thomas Scaife was a bank engine driver, Joseph Rutherford was works foreman; and the engine which blew up was not a Norris but a tank engine, unusual enough in appearance to attract the attention of the two men as it rested in Bromsgrove after its day's work on 10 November 1840. Its crew, John Inshaw and son Paul, obligingly

Headstones to Scaife and Rutherford, Bromsgrove, blown up by the Surprise

stepped down to let Scaife and Rutherford have a closer look and without warning the engine, only too appropriately named *Surprise*, blew up. The engine carved on Rutherford's stone is one of the Norrises, while Scaife's memorial, Rev W Awdry concludes, probably shows the *Boston*. From time to time it has been argued that the masons responsible for these two stones made a couple of awful mistakes: neither of the engines they sketched was the one that blew up and there appears to be a discrepancy about the date of the disaster. It's not difficult, however, to exonerate them. Better by far, surely, to carve the engine the men worked with and were familiar with rather than the stranger that blew them to bits; and though Scaife died outright, Rutherford lingered on until the following day.

Rutherford's stone has stood for a year longer than Scaife's, erected in 1841 by his widow and bearing a conventional verse which warns the reader about the speedy passage of time. A year later Scaife's fellow workers had got the money together to commemorate him in equal style and to include a verse twice as long and since much quoted:

My *engine* now is cold and still,
No water does my *boiler* fill;
My *coke* affords its flame no more,
My days of usefulness are o'er.
My *wheels* deny their wonted speed,
No more my guiding hands they heed;
My *whistle*, too, has lost its tune,
Its shrill and thrilling sounds are gone;
My *valves* are now thrown open wide,
My *flanges* all refuse to guide,
My *clacks*, also, tho' once so strong,
Refuse to aid the busy throng.
No more I feel each urging breath,
My *steam* is now condensed in death.
Life's *railway* o'er, each station past,
In death I'm stopped and rest at last.
Farewell, dear friends, and cease to weep,
In Christ I'm SAFE, in Him I sleep.

An 'unknown Friend' wrote this and strictly speaking it may be an original epitaph for one of the railway era's earliest victims: the play on Scaife's name in the last line would suggest that. But it looks as though it owes a lot in style and inspiration to other widely used verses to those in trade, like the blacksmith, Thomas Cole, at White Ladies Aston, who died in 1807:

My sledge and hammer lie reclining
My bellows to have lost their wind,
My fire extinguished, forge decayed
And in the dust my vice is laid
My coal is spent my iron gone
My last nail driven, my work is done

This particular epitaph crops up all over the place and can be seen, for example (though only now in part as much of it has worn away) on the stone to Richard Stephens, a blacksmith from Lowesmoor Wharf, who died in 1831 and is buried in Claines. And this silencing of tools at a man's death is a common image in epitaphs to those who may be said to have had 'noisy' jobs. The following inscription appears on the headstone of William Bluck, for 49 years 'woodman' to the Earls of Coventry, buried at Grafton Flyford in 1872:

> Twas stern disease his footsteps staid:
> And down the woodman's axe was laid,
> No more the forest feared his stroke;
> He fell as falls the rugged oak.
> And like that rugged oak must lie
> Till called to judgment in the sky.
> There shall he find his name above
> Welcomed and ... (The rest is illegible)

Domestic servants are heavily represented throughout the county's churchyards, their bodies laid to rest under stones set up by their former employers, emphasising the latter's responsibility towards their extended family. Some of these headstones are quite specific and serve to underline the hierarchy which existed in the servant world, for you were very much more likely to have your precise job engraved on your headstone if you attended to the more personal needs of your employer or looked after his or her land. So among a number of gravestones to servants in Kempsey we have a butler — John Helme who died in 1853 after 36 years of service in the Nuttall family, having gained 'the most unreserved confidence of his master'. Among an equal number of servants' graves in Croome D'Abitot churchyard, on the former estate of the Earls of Coventry, a valet, John Chance, is commended by the eighth earl for his honesty during a 25-year service. Unlike some gravestones to servants whose wording and size of lettering make you wonder just who is being honoured, the poor deceased or the surviving grand employer, John's headstone shows a degree of care and affection on the part of his employer.

> He expired at the Star Inn Oxford and was not left to lie in a strange town but he was brought to this church yard out of respect to his memory by his master the present earl. (He) had served His Majesty George the 3rd in 11th Dragoons in Egypt and he was as ... honest ... (The last couple of lines lie buried as well)

Croome D'Abitot is that churchyard in Worcestershire which best gives some idea of the very different world which disappeared not that many decades ago. The church itself is now redundant, maintained by the Redundant Churches Fund; but from its main entrance there is a splendid view over the fields which slope down to Croome Court, across which the earl's household must have ridden or walked to church; and in the churchyard are buried the servants and family who worked and lived on this large estate — not side by side, though, for the latter's tombs are to be found south of the church.

In Birtsmorton churchyard, one of the county's most isolated and standing next to the beautiful and restored Birtsmorton Court, there is a headstone to 'Eliz Beale Late housekeeper to LORD BELLAMOUNT near 30 years and wife of Peter Beale Steward to the above LORD who died June 15. 1810 Aged 96 Yrs'. Presumably she was looked after in her old age — but note whose name is in capital letters.

Nurses and nannies were also vital members of large households, especially in periods when parents preferred only brief encounters with children who had been washed, clothed and fed. One wonders what Ann Nash who died at 86 in 1857 had to put up with, for her gravestone describes her as 'for many

IN Memory of
Eliz Beale Late Housekeeper
to LORD BELLAMOUNT
near thirty years and wife of
Peter Beale Steward to the
above LORD who died June
15. 1810
Aged 96 yrs

*In memory of a Birtsmorton
housekeeper, Elizabeth Beale*

Eleanor Hibble's rare wooden memorial at Madresfield

years a faithful and unwearied Nurse to the late Mr Phipps of Bricklehampton'. Still, whatever it was he showed his gratefulness by having the stone put up. In Madresfield there is a sturdy wooden memorial, very unusual in this county, to Eleanor Hibble, 'a faithful nurse', almost certainly at the Court next door to the churchyard as she lies alongside the Beauchamp family graves.

As well as the Shrawley gamekeeper mentioned above there are others at Hampton Lovett where James Simons' headstone was erected in 1856 by his employer at Westwood Park 'as a tribute to his integrity and worth' having served as gamekeeper, then bailiff for 25 years; at Ombersley, on the Sandys estate, where the stone to Joseph Wright, head gamekeeper to Lord Sandys for 17 years, was erected in 1882 in an area containing a group of graves of the staff at Ombersley Court; and at Pirton where another Coventry servant, John Corbett, died in 1910 and lies beneath a very nice headstone whose top section and edges are decorated with flowers and leaves in relief, some small recognition for his 42 years of service.

And there were those, of course, who laboured in the beloved gardens of the great houses — William Mason (died 1822) 43 years on the Overbury estate of the Martin family; James Hughes, buried in 1873 at Salwarpe, after 35 years at High Park; and George Reynolds who died in 1859 in Wribbenhall and is buried in Stourport. 50 of his 69 years were spent tending the gardens of a Mrs Soly of Sandbourne House, near Bewdley. 'He was a truly honest man and his end was peace.'

It is worth remembering that domestic servants accounted for a significant proportion of the labour force in centuries past and, as well as those in great households, many would be working in families and houses surprisingly small by our standards. Comparatively few therefore would have had a headstone and of those who were buried in more style most would have been described in only the most general of terms, 'faithful servant' the

Richard Howell, Martley: fifty years service in the house of Foley

most popular phrase. These were usually the real domestics who cleaned and washed and did most of the donkey work. But the precise nature of their work often leaves us just guessing. Elisabeth Cooper who died at Claines in 1859 was 'a faithful servant for 56 years to M A V'. What kind of a servant and who was 'M A V'? And what was the position of Richard Howell who died in 1800 after 50 years service to no less than four heads of another of the county's great families, the Foleys? He is buried at Martley, described as 'Sincere in his Friendship, true to his trust, a good Christian'; and his headstone is a wonderful example of a mason's difficulties with spacing, punctuation and abbreviation.

Just occasionally a heartfelt tribute, if a little sugary to today's reader, survives to the largely anonymous army of manual servants.

From early Infancy she lived under the Protection of one Family in this her Native Parish until her decease, being her first and only earthly service. In this humble walk of Life she was justly esteemed for her fidelity and diligence and a Generosity of Temper, anxious to promote the Comfort and Happiness of every one. Loving her neighbours as herself. That Singleness of Heart discoverable in her Actions, was greatly strengthned and imbued with early habits of Piety producing the peaceful fruits of Holiness.

Such was the summing up of the life of Mary Osborne, 44 when she died at Finstall in 1815. Her large stone which could not have been cheap was erected by 'A B' and renewed 27 years later by 'R B'. It is distinctly possible that these initials refer to the Brettle family who paid for the chapel of St Godwald's to be completely rebuilt in 1772. Clearly, the feelings expressed were not just empty words.

Cecilia Denley was 99 when she died in 1895: perhaps she was a former governess or housekeeper as her stone at Croome D'Abitot was erected by the Earl and Countess of Coventry, Viscount Deerhurst and the Honourables Reginald and Charles. And Edward Davis was for '49 years and 11 months a faithful servant' to the Wheeler family at Newnham Court before being buried at Knighton-on-Teme in 1869. He had spent almost three-quarters of his life at the Court.

The traditional professions of the church, law and army are well represented as are surgeons, a little lower in the social scale. Clergymen are instantly recognisable by the title and by the frequent references to their length of service in this or that parish; they also seemed to have had the edge over others in claiming the prime spot outside the east end of the church. While most are decidedly formal there is one that cannot help but raise a smile and that, together with the fact that the body in question was buried in the churchyard, would seem sufficient justification for inclusion, despite the memorial being *inside* the church. The gentleman in question was Rev W A Pruen BD, curate of Fladbury for 27 years and afterwards vicar of

Snitterfield. The memorial just inside the church at Fladbury reads:

> He received his death stroke while in the pulpit at the Archdeacon's Visitation at Stratford-on-Avon June 1st 1840 in the 58th year of his Age. His last words bespoke the zeal in his service of his God, and the warmth of heart towards his brethren.
> 'The Lord pardon this neglect of duty! May the God of peace be with you.'

after which, clearly affected by the suddenness of the vicar's departure, the memorial writer inscribed

> "Therefore be ye also ready"

It is not only Anglican clergy who are buried in Church of England churchyards, of course. It has long been the law that everyone (even dissenting ministers!) has the right to be buried in their local Anglican churchyard except, in the past, the unbaptised, the excommunicated, executed criminals and those pronounced guilty of taking their own lives. The latter group was allowed burial in an unconsecrated part of the churchyard from 1823 and strictly speaking, though suicide is no longer a criminal offence, this remains the position in ecclesiastical law. In practice normal burial takes place.

In Broadway a nineteenth-century Congregational minister lies buried in St Eadburgha's; and lying on the ground at Bromsgrove is the headstone to Joshua Peart, the Baptist minister, whose cracked and incomplete memorial is still able to tell anyone interested that somewhere in the vicinity were buried Peart's wives — Mary (1795), Susanna (1814) and Leonora (1819). The minister himself lived on to 1825, though only church records can provide these details as the bottom line of the stone is defaced. The Baptists didn't have much time for the notion of consecrated ground, yet the very first census of 1801 revealed that most of them were buried in Anglican churchyards.

Other servants of the church whose contributions are recorded include organists, and a 'Scripture Reader' buried at Whittington, a man called James Riley who died in 1894. But by far the largest group of lay people associated with the work of the parish is that of those important people, the parish clerks. For sheer length of service they are as a breed unbeatable.

At Rushock there are stones to two men — John Jackson and William Clark — who between them served the parish for most of the nineteenth century and at Stoulton similar inscriptions show that a father and son did likewise, son Benjamin dying at 92 in 1912 after 60 years as parish clerk, his father William Simmonds serving in the same capacity for 'many years' before him. Stoulton seemed to breed stability: Richard Henry Loxley was church warden there for nearly 50 years. Once in office, it would seem, many gave a lifetime of service: William Freeman at Grimley died in 1879 aged 92, parish clerk for 60 years; William Barnard at Badsey died in 1892 after 50 years service; Joseph Gwynne at Catshill died in 1909 after 40 years service; Samuel Knight of Harvington died in 1829 after 46 years service; Edmund Salisbury of Little Comberton died in 1911 after 57 years service. The same dedication existed in the nonconformist churches. There may not be parish clerks but there are deacons and one of them, George Frederick Bomford, served at Atch Lench for 68 years. All these men died in their 80s and 90s — the work must have agreed with them.

After the cleric and the parish clerk comes the schoolteacher, though not every village had one. In the first half of the nineteenth century a number of members of the profession were exposed by people like George Griffiths (buried at Ribbesford) as neglectful and often verging on the illiterate; but those from the latter decades were quite different and the respect and affection they earned comes through in the wording on their gravestones.

> This stone is erected by his late pupils and friends in testimony of their regard and good feeling towards him while living, and of their deep regret at his demise. He was for 27 years master of Grafton Flyford Parish School and was a most useful man in parish matters, always ready to assist when his services were needed. The tables of commandments were placed in the church by him and were the work of his hands.

This heartfelt tribute is to Peter Akers. The date of his death is unfortunately no longer readable. Similar feelings are expressed on a tombstone at Lickey, not to the local teacher but to Rachel Ann Hoyland who was born in Kendal and died at Hillcrest, The Lickey, in 1893. The inscription reads: 'This stone is erected by the Members of Class IX of the Severn Street Schools, Birmingham in loving remembrance of Mrs Hoyland's work amongst them and their wives'. There's nothing to tell us why she died at the relatively early age of 39, nor why in particular the wives of her former scholars should want to be especially mentioned. Perhaps she taught at the Severn Street First Day Adult Schools, founded in 1845 by Joseph Sturge, the Quaker reformer; though it is strange that in a list of teachers which is included in an anniversary account of 1895 Mrs Hoyland does not appear but John William Hoyland does. Perhaps she is there under her maiden name, perhaps she wasn't a teacher at all but the terribly helpful wife of one. Whatever she was, whatever she did, there were clearly a lot of people who appreciated her.

The mention of her birthplace as though she were a foreigner is interesting and there are numerous examples of this throughout the county, for even late in the last century not being born in the parish was noteworthy. The stone of Mary Corbett, for example, a waiter (*sic*) at the Commercial George Hotel, Droitwich, who died there in 1842 and is buried in St Peter's churchyard, refers to her as coming from Lichfield; but more unusual is the wording on a Kempsey gravestone to one Armand Richer 'a Norman by birth of respectable parentage' who 'passed thirty-five years in the Family of the Reverend John Neate who in gratitude for his long and faithful services have erected this Stone in testimony of his work'.

In the same churchyard Richard Jarvis, another 'foreigner' (from Eccleshall, Staffordshire) has a stone erected 'in affectionate remembrance by his Scholars and Friends'. He must have made his mark quickly for Richard, who combined teaching with organ-playing, was only 23 when he died in 1870. At Bredon's Norton Jane Leworthy, for many years village schoolmistress, must have been quite something for she it is who gets main billing on the headstone while her husband William is described simply as 'husband of the above'. Both died in the 1920s. But one of the county's longest serving teachers lies buried in the little churchyard of St Mary's Catholic Church at Harvington. Joseph Ilsley was the 'faithful and respected schoolmaster' for 43 years. He must have started as a teenager since he was only 60 when he died in 1874. Can this evident respect for the teacher have anything to do with the sheer length of time so many of them spent in the same post, enabling them over the years to make their mark by becoming central figures in the community through their close knowledge of the people and the place?

The existence of an early charity school at Ombersley is marked by a stone, dated 1771, to 'John Williams, Staff Master at Mr LLOYD's Charity School'. The school, housed in a building opposite the Ombersley Gallery, was founded in 1729 to instruct poorer children in English, writing, reading and arithmetic.

Oh stay at home, my lad, and plough
The land and not the sea,
And leave the soldiers at their drill,
And all about the idle hill
Shepherd your sheep with me.

Oh stay with company and mirth
And daylight and the air;
Too full already is the grave
Of fellows that were good and brave
And died because they were.

A E Housman *Last Poems*

Although there are many graves to servicemen and women in the county it is not easy to determine what they did. Sometimes a word like 'stoker' or 'pilot' will appear but normally only the rank and regiment or service. And of course many references to officer rank on headstones may simply mean that the title continued to be used in civilian life. The best accounts — unfortunately, for the purposes of this book — are usually to be found on plaques inside churches which give lengthy descriptions of service around the world: a major at White Ladies Aston who as a young officer attended the internment on St Helena of Napoleon I; a veteran in the same church who enjoyed ' brief intervals of repose during 53 years amidst the varied fortunes of a soldier's life'.

But in the church or in the churchyard the inscriptions amount to a catalogue of British involvement in wars all over the world, some we know about, others whose obscurity just makes us wonder why. What an environmental shock it must have been for the country village lads who went to fight. And how sad it is to look at a churchyard like tiny Besford's and see several memorials to those who died in France in the 1914 – 18 War; or to read at Salwarpe that 58 died in the same war 'for King and

Country'; or, further back, to stand in Tenbury Wells' churchyard and read on the Handley family's stone that William died in camp before Sebastapol on 26 January 1855 in his 29th year. Was this a result of injuries or did he succumb to the diseases that abounded in camp and carried off so many including 23-year-old Corporal Arthur Philip Hodgetts who died of enteric fever at Kroonstad while fighting in the Boer War and is buried at Wyre Piddle?

It is interesting to contrast the Handley family headstone whose brief inscriptions to several members suggest only modest prosperity with that of another young man, a few miles away at Bretforton, who was also at Sebastapol in 1855. The memorial tablet to Lieutenant James Collins Ashwin, son of James Ashwin Esquire, is set into the outside of the church's east wall and details how he died — 'in the assault on the great Redan June 18 1855' — and then explains how the monument and memorial window were erected by public subscription to perpetuate the memory of a soldier whose gallantry and bearing his commanding officer had recorded.

A number of headstones have survived to those in the retail trade. William Perkins, 'Late Hairdresser of the City of Worcester' was buried at Tardebigge in 1825; Rueben Smith, a florist, who died in 1897, lies in the churchyard of St Nicholas, Kemerton; and at Clent there is one of those wonderfully flowery epitaphs to a highly successful draper, John Harris:

He was an eminent mercer,
And draper in Stourbridge,
Where by the blessing of
Almighty God
On his industry and integrity,
He acquired an ample fortune,
And enjoyed many years,
Independent.

Distinguished through life,
For his charity benevolence,
And true patriotism;
He bequeathed his wealth
To increase the comforts
Of many.
He died a bachelor
July 31st 1843
In his seventy-second year.

It goes without saying that there are publicans all over the place, reminders of times gone by when there were very many more pubs than there are today (87 licensed premises, for instance, in Bewdley in the middle of the last century). But an awful lot of their headstones have disappeared in recent decades and it is a pity that the best one of all, though still standing, has worn almost beyond readability. In its prime the upper section showed various bowls, bottles and pots which Richard Philpotts, publican of the Bell, Belbroughton would have used daily until he died in 1766 and the cheering verse below *used* to read:

To tell a merry or a wondrous tale,
Over a cheerful glass of nappy ale,
In harmless mirth, was his supreme delight —
To please his guests or friends by day or night.
But no fine tale, how well soever told,
Could make the tyrant Death his stroke withhold.
That fatal stroke has laid him here in dust,
To rise again once more with joy we trust.

In a county like Worcestershire one might have expected to have found quite a number of gravestones to those involved in the building and operating of the canals and railways. A few have been mentioned earlier and there are others; but there are less than might have been anticipated. On the other hand, perhaps expectations are too high: many of the workers would not have risen to a headstone and at least some of those involved in early accidents during the excavation and building stages would presumably have been taken home to be buried.

There is of course a much older means of transport in Worcestershire — the River Severn, until a century and a half ago one of the world's most important commercial highways. Watermen sailed up and down the river carrying all sorts of cargo and negotiating the inland ports of Bewdley, Worcester and Upton-on-Severn. Along the Severn were a number of ferries; the one at Hampstall could be dangerous and nine people lost their lives there when the ferry capsized in 1919. How dramatic, though, must have been the storm nearly a century earlier when on 23 December 1821 John Oakes, son of John Oakes, waterman, lost his life. His epitaph at Ribbesford is now a little worn but enough survives to convey the nature of his death:

> Borea's blast and Neptune's waves
> Have tost me to & fro
> I strove as I could my life to save
> At last obliged to go
> Now at an anchor ...
> When many of the fleet ...
> But now once more I ... (the rest illegible)

In the same churchyard the verse on John Robinson's headstone of 1821 reads:

> For many a wet and windy night and day
> Through Severn's dangerous course I made my way,
> Full forty years in friendship's trusty Bark,

Guided by Providence through light and dark.
With future hopes of being for ever blest,
So my dear friends adieu
Here I lie at rest

He must have started work on the Severn when he was 14.

Some gravestones are vivid reminders of jobs that have long
ceased to exist — 'Parish Maltster' at Claines (Richard Norton
who died in 1714), the 'Plough Wright' at Harvington (Joseph
Knight who died in 1834), the currier at Frankley, John Taylor,
lately working in Piccadilly, whose stone is the only one in this
family group to achieve 'Mr' status — he must have done well,
the apothecary at Bretforton, Thomas Ashwin, who when he
died at the goodly age of 79 was still referred to as son of ...! At
St Andrew and St Mary de Witton, Droitwich, John Brown is
buried, a zealous 'Collector of the Salt Duties' for 32 years who,

The much respected village hawker, Ishmael James, at Welland

hard to believe, died 'much regretted' in 1791. And there is a touching epitaph at Welland to a tinker, Ishmael James, and his wife Lilo who chose where to be buried, it is said, by throwing a stone in the air and taking the plot where it landed:

> For many years a familiar figure over the whole countryside, as a village hawker, his honorable ways making him respected by all who knew him, he died at Tetbury May 7th 1908, aged 78 years.

Sometimes it is just that the job has been 'rationalised'. At Beckford there is a stone to Benjamin Dyer and his wife Sarah who died in 1838: 'She was the daily letter carrier from Beckford to Tewkesbury for nineteen years: and having walked about 16 miles a day during that period is supposed to have walked about 90,000 Miles'. And sometimes headstones make us realise how attitudes and values have changed. These days, for instance, working for public service companies does not provide *quite* the same amount of pride and satisfaction that it did in the last century when Philip Greenway was buried at Claines, 23 years engineer to the 'Worcester Water Works' and 'much and deservedly respected', and Francis Harris was buried in the same decade at Feckenham, 'for twenty-two years a greatly respected servant of the London and North Western Railway Company'. And would today's Inspector of Taxes particularly want his profession carved in stone as William Rance did when he was buried at Malvern Priory in 1842?

Surprisingly few stones to craftsmen have survived. As well as those already mentioned there are one or two carpenters and workers in wood; several stonemasons — at Bredon's Norton and South Littleton, for instance; a cooper at Ombersley; 'An Honest Man and a Good Bricklayer', Thomas Cooper, at Alvechurch (probably more remembered now because he was a member of the Shakespeare Players, an amateur group going strong in the last century, and his stone was erected by fellow

Shakespearians); and a watchmaker at Pershore whose memorial commendably avoids all tempting cliches involving Father Time and scythes and hourglasses. If craftsmen aren't thick on the ground the unskilled are thinner still, the exception being William Copstone (see Chapter Two).

Even so, it still amounts to much more than we get from the headstones of this century when the only occupational references are usually to those who have earned a living in some rather specialised work — artists, at Eckington and Pirton, a diplomat at Norton and Lenchwick, and a certain well-known composer at Malvern Wells.

4 Mysteries and surprises

On a dull and chilly day in early March two gravediggers paused for a rest. One stood shoulder deep in one of several freshly dug holes, a great burly fellow, chest bare, head shaven; the other gazed down from the grave's edge, silent and serious. There should have been hulks, this was pure Dickens. Instead there were two pale fold-away plastic chairs, set out for a tea break perhaps. For this was the little churchyard of Ipsley, 1992, and these were freelance gravediggers from Staffordshire, digging holes to rehouse bones from the other side of the church where building was due to start. Worcestershire churchyards are full of surprises.

To begin with there is the lady who appears to have lived till she was 309. Sara Charlett's headstone stands just to the south of the church tower in Cleeve Prior. The fairly primitive lettering shows that she 'departed this life 6th day of October Anno Dom 1693 Aged ...' and it *looks* like 309. The middle figure is raised a little: did the mason start the '9' and then decide it was too close to the '3'? Nearby there is another headstone and another little conundrum, this one to Alice Bennet 'Who Died May the 130th 1719 Aged 17'. Was this the work of the same mason? Was his '0' here a gigantic full stop or was the first stroke superfluous? Maybe he was just fond of carving circles.

Then there is the Feckenham man, John Collier, who seems to have died twice, firstly on 6 June and then again a fortnight later:

He died on the 6th and 20th day of June an dom 1671 Being aged 40

Presumably, this is just a reflection of the ringing tones of the inscription writer — or the mason.

Two much more genuine puzzles have absolutely nothing to do with the style of the mason and must rank amongst the most curious memorials in the country. The first is at Bayton, a churchyard tucked away down a lane, a manor house and farm opposite the entrance, with lovely rolling scenery to the far side. Affixed to the south wall of the chancel is a rectangular slab, cracked but perfectly readable, its cod Latin suggesting that if you lead a righteous life you will have nothing to fear in death.

Cod Latin at Bayton

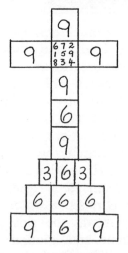

Numerical poser: Rev Hooper's cross, Upton Warren

Though it is now hard to discern the Professor of Classics at Durham University recently confirmed that the date right at the bottom is 1654 (given in the Victoria County History). But what is the memorial doing there in the first place?

The parish registers of the period are no help but over the years there have been various theories: that the stone was to someone who 'disappeared' during the Commonwealth, a supporter of the Stuarts; that the initials 'T(?J)M' at the bottom mean there must be some connection with the Meysey family, lords of the manor of Shakenhurst from the fourteenth century. Last year Peter Wardle wrote a couple of pieces about the strange stone in the parish magazine but the responses were disappointingly unconvincing. So the mystery remains and in the absence of any real evidence we have to admit we do not know who was responsible for the memorial, what its purpose was and where it might have been before its present position (because it looks like the horizontal top of a tomb). But the date is very tantalising: 3 September 1654 was exactly three years to the day after the battle of Worcester when the forces of the future Charles II were routed by Cromwell's much larger army.

Peter Wardle also has a view — that at some stage during the Commonwealth when churchyards were frowned upon a local chap (but certainly not a craftsman for the grammar is bad, the letter 'N' is back to front and the lettering is not much more than scratched) roughly copied a Latin inscription, added a date and initials and thus produced an unofficial memorial to a relative or friend. He admits, though, he could be wrong.

The second teaser is very different for the clergyman responsible bequeathed to posterity page after page of explanation. Still, we are not left much the wiser. In Upton Warren there is a white marble cross, mounted on a stone base of three steps, to the Hooper family, Rev F J B Hooper, rector for 52 years, his wife Caroline and their children. The front of the memorial is a little cluttered, with the rector's biographical

details — including, oddly, the date 1881 though Hooper
ministered there until his death in 1888 — biblical references, a
Latin adage, the episcopal symbol, some Greek inscribed
sideways down the shaft of the cross and the Christian symbol of
the fish in the centre of the transverse, to the left, right and
above it the five initial letters of the Greek for 'Jesus Christ, Son
of God, Saviour' (which make up the word fish). It is the back of
the cross, however, where many would not necessarily think of
looking, that makes this memorial quite unique.

Rev Hooper was clearly obsessed with numbers and must have
decided well in advance the exact form his memorial was to take
because he went to the trouble to explain the symbolism in his
book *The Revelation Expounded*. The middle letter of the Greek
word for fish, for example, 'has the numerical value of 9, or the
square of 3, the number of the Trinity on the central point of the
cross'. The other strand in his argument rests on the tenet that
18 (666) is the mark of 'the Beast' and since five of the six
additions on the pedestal, totalled up and across, amount to 18,
the cross, or the kingdom of Christ, can be seen to trample on
the pedestal of his adversary, the Devil.

The top step of the pedestal has worn rather badly in the last
decade and the stylised drawing is based on information
recorded in the late 70s. It would be a great pity if this
amazingly eccentric product of a mind fascinated by the
translation of biblical themes into numerical symbols was
allowed simply to crumble away.

Another Worcestershire churchyard mystery is to be found
not far away at St Mary de Wyche in Wychbold. Lying in the
grass in the north-west of the churchyard is a stone, shaped like a
fat bottle, which says simply:

> In memory of fifty infants gathered unto their Saviour's bosom.

There is no date but it is probably from the latter decades of the
nineteenth century or the very early years of this, comparatively

recent enough for there still to be someone somewhere who knows its story; but enquiries made in the parish have drawn a blank and an examination of the registers and burial plan has revealed no reference to the stone.

'Fifty infants' are a lot of children and any particular tragedy of that scale would surely have been recorded and become a familiar part of the area's history. So speculation inevitably takes over. The church is not much more than a century old — was the stone put there at that time by someone or some group who wanted to commemorate the deaths of little children who had died over a period of time and never had a gravestone between them, children perhaps from nearby Stoke Prior where John Corbett's great salt works employed so many? Or did someone want to record the deaths of stillborn babies, again over a period of time, who had been buried unsung in one or more of the other churches in the area? We may never know.

We should at some stage get to know what the United Ancient Order of Druids got — or even gets — up to. There are several headstones in the Bewdley area to members of this organisation and from them we gather there were a number of lodges which met at pubs like the Union Inn and the Malt Shovel. Among those buried at Ribbesford are John Millward who died in 1883 and whose stone was erected by the members of Lodge 466; Richard Millward who died six years later and whose memorial was erected by the 'Brothers of Lodge 258'; and John Robinson who died in 1821, a member of the Order which met at the Union Inn. The ancient order is mentioned only on headstones in the Bewdley area and why there appears to be no knowledge of its activities there is a mystery. The only suggestion so far is that the Druids might have been rather like the Independent Order of Oddfellows, a secret fraternal and benevolent society founded in England in the eighteenth century, or the Royal Ancient Order of the Buffaloes, but with a distinctive religious side to it associated with Stonehenge.

Not all Worcestershire's churchyard curiosities are mysteries yet to be fathomed. Some are simply surprising, like the stretch of sandstone wall, some 20 feet long, which stands at the south-west edge of the pretty churchyard at Areley Kings. It must be one of the country's most unlikely looking memorials, passed no doubt by countless visitors unaware of the story. On it in large plain, though faded, letters is the following inscription:

LITHOLOGEMA QUARE?
REPONITUR SIR HARRY

which Noake loosely interpreted as

Wherefore this heap of stones?
Why, to cover Sir Harry's bones.

Sir Harry Coningsby was a Hertfordshire man who is said to have died of a broken heart as a result of accidentally letting his

Sir Harry's wall memorial at Areley Kings

child, with whom he was playing at an open window, fall into the moat and drown. He became a recluse, ending his days in Areley; and when he died in 1701 he left instructions that the children of the parish were to have the walnuts from the tree planted over his grave and crack them open on his gravestone. The tree was cut down in the early nineteenth century by one of the rectors.

Just inside the churchyard at Huddington, to the right of the lychgate, is a very simple wooden cross to Keturah Isabella Davidson who died in 1903. No-one would have expected her grave to be of interest to any beyond her family. But many people must have seen it during this century, remarking no doubt on her unusual Christian name; for only a few yards away is Huddington Court, a centre of catholicism for generations. Here some of the leading conspirators of the Gunpowder Plot lived and planned with others to blow up Parliament; and here a fugitive from the battle of Worcester must have sought a safe place to hide, his remains marked by a crucifix of oak and bronze, set in an alcove of clipped yew, immediately behind Keturah Davidson's wooden memorial.

> Nearby when digging the grave of Keturah Davidson in 1903 were found the remains of an unknown man who from the fact that with him were Scots coins of King James VI and King Charles I and a French coin of Louis XIII, a double turnois dated 1637, is believed to have been a fugitive from the Royal Army defeated at Worcester on 3rd September 1651

Sometimes there are tombstones which look as though they should be somewhere else. At Bromsgrove an ancient stone effigy of an unknown lady lies in the churchyard near the north doorway. She is clearly out of place, used to better things, and the outdoor life has not suited her. She began life inside the church but was dug up from the north aisle and placed on one of the windowsills. She was not allowed to rest, however, but turfed out over a century ago so that features worn then are now quite obliterated. A few miles south at St Peter de Witton, Droitwich, there is an unusual item fixed to the outside wall of the south transept. It is a stone coffin lid which has been attributed to a thirteenth-century prior of Studley for the priory held the living of the church until the Dissolution. It is easy to miss as it blends so well with the church masonry, looking at a distance like a small buttress.

Then there are the stones that are normal in every way except for some unusual detail, like the initials 'W R' and 'M R' on the end of a tomb at Broadway, not of those within — William and Mary Dickin — but of another William and Mary, King and Queen of England; and the first four bars of 'I know that my Redeemer liveth' from Handel's *Messiah* which appear on the late eighteenth-century headstone to Richard Hussey, clerk to

Richard Hussey's musical headstone at Hanbury

the parish of Hanbury and 'Father of the musical Society'. The lettering on this latter stone is of a high standard and it would be a tragedy if the face of this very interesting memorial were allowed to deteriorate any further.

Sometimes the unexpected has nothing to do with a tomb or headstone for there are other things that can catch the eye in a churchyard. At Madresfield, for example, there is a very attractive well which is set on steps and has a wrought-iron canopy. At Elmley Castle are two of the more unusual of the county's many sundials, both dating from the sixteenth century, the westerly one bearing the arms of the Savage family on its north face. Both have undergone changes since they were first made and twenty years ago, when almost all traces of their original iron gnomons had disappeared, new ones of copper, bronze and steel were fitted. Sundials were in widespread use during the middle ages and portable versions were being manufactured throughout the eighteenth century. But they were only ever of use during sunshine and daylight and when the Elmley Castle dials were first introduced public clocks had already been telling the time in England for nearly 150 years.

In two Worcestershire villages it is possible to see reminders of the times when churchyards were anything but peaceful places. On the buttress to the tower on the south wall of Cleeve Prior church are indentations, clearly visible, where centuries ago men sharpened their arrows in preparation for bow-and-arrow practice which often took place in the churchyard itself; and on the north side of the chancel wall at Rock is a very obvious series of grooves which, according to the writer of the village's history, were made by the Welsh hero Owen Glendower in 1405 while preparing for battle against the English on Woodbury Hill.

And so, finally, to a horse, one of the most unexpected sights in Worcestershire. Not strictly in a churchyard but in the grounds right next to one, there is a headstone at Madresfield

The effects of medieval arrow-sharpening at Cleeve Prior

Court which marks the grave of Shadrach, ridden by Lord
Raglan in the Crimean War. The faithful charger survived that
encounter (though his master, of course, was usually watching
from positions of safety) only to be killed not long afterwards in
a hunting accident. The grounds at Madresfield are not open to
the public but it is possible to see Shadrach's mound on August
Bank Holidays when the Court holds its agricultural show.

5 Fame: short-lived, longlasting

It has already been stressed that in no sense is this a 'who-is-buried-where' guide to the county nor a gazetteer of notables. But the manner in which these worthies are memorialised is certainly of interest. They do however raise a problem because their social status meant that most were accorded burial places *inside* the church. Hence the excavation of crypts and vaults to receive such august remains and the subsequent stench which arose (literally), not to mention the weakening of church floors as stone slabs were lifted and replaced. Some of the more remarkable memorials therefore cannot be the province of this book, though very occasionally the rule is relaxed when it is clear that the interior epitaph refers to a churchyard burial.

This is the case with a remarkable woman who chose to decline the honourable burial place for which her social position would have qualified her. In 1630 when she died Meriel Lyttleton, daughter of the Lord Chancellor of England, was buried at St John the Baptist, at the gates of Hagley Hall:

And by Express direction in her will,
Was interr'd among her *Poor Neighbours* in this churchyard
Under a plain Stone whereon not even her Name is inscribed.

And so she rested for the best part of a century and a half. Until along came a descendant, the Bishop of Carlisle, who thought he knew better and caused a plaque to be put in the church describing her worth and work. She probably turned in her grave but we are grateful to be able to read her story. Her husband had been imprisoned in the Tower where he had died in 1601 for his part in the rebellion led by the Earl of Essex against Elizabeth I. For this error he had forfeited his estates. Singlehandedly she procured the return of the estates by petitioning James I in person as he journeyed to London to ascend the throne. Mistress Lyttleton proceeded to pay off most of her husband's debts and lived 'frugally but charitably'. Years later and long after anyone could have known her the family recorded its no doubt heartfelt thanks.

Emma Vernon's grave is another well away from its expected position. It stands at the northern edge of Hanbury's vast churchyard, rectangular, plain and slightly odd-looking with a brief inscription which could well be overlooked. But the words 'and was by her own desire buried here' clearly speak volumes. She had inherited Hanbury Hall and then married, probably in compliance with her mother's wishes for a grand catch, Henry Cecil, nephew and heir to the Earl of Exeter. Cecil, according to Dr Treadway Nash, drove his young wife to drink and the valium equivalent of the day and thirteen years later Emma left (with the consumptive curate with whom she had fallen in love). Within four years the curate was dead; but Emma married for a third time, living with her husband, John Phillips, first near Bewdley, then back at Hanbury Hall (when Henry Cecil died) until she died in 1818. At her death she was wrapped in the sheet that had covered her curate's body 25 years earlier. Did her decision to be buried away from the Vernon sepulchre arise from any feeling of unworthiness or could she simply no longer see the point?

A century or so later another member of the family was particular about his burial place. The last baronet, Sir George Vernon, died in 1940. Despite being chairman of the parish council he was fairly neurotic in his dislike of the Church of England and each year refused to pay his tithes without a great performance. When he shot himself at the beginning of the Second World War his request to be buried in Shrawley Wood, on another of his estates, was honoured. Near the Court at Madresfield stands a Celtic cross bearing only a date: 19 February 1891. It was the only form of commemoration the 6th Earl Beauchamp would allow and his body lies in the churchyard in an unmarked grave.

In many churchyards there exist groups of memorials to

Memorial grandeur: 1st Baron Hindlip's tomb at Hindlip

members of the same family who may be buried beneath in a family vault. These underground chambers are easy to overlook although one at Salwarpe is marked by a headstone indicating where entry can be effected via steps; some may have iron railings around them though in numerous cases these have been taken away. In World War Two, for example, such metal was collected to be recycled for munitions. A variety of vaults can be seen in the county. Sometimes the vault may take the form of a stone chest, sometimes it is fully underground with slabs on top giving details of who has been interred. In the little churchyard at Hindlip is a very large and opulent-looking vault in the form of a catafalque with what could have been shields down the sides onto which have been carved the names and dates of those buried. The memorial is to the first Baron Hindlip and his family, whose considerable fortune was based on the working man's drink. As plain — but wealthy — Henry Allsopp, he had taken over from his father as head of the brewery firm in Burton-on-Trent when quite a young man. In 1860 he bought Hindlip Manor and from 1874 to 1880 represented East Worcestershire in parliament. He failed to get re-elected but presumably being created a baron was some compensation. When he died just over 100 years ago he left the Hindlip estate and other land in Worcestershire and Derbyshire to his eldest son, the second baron, and a vast amount of money to the rest of his family. Just to the side of the little church, incidentally, is probably the most unlikely building to house the grizzly exhibits of a police museum — a delightful fourteenth-century half-timbered structure.

One of the most attractive and varied churchyards in the county is that of St Bartholomew's at Tardebigge. It is interesting to see that unlike Hindlip and Croome D'Abitot, for example, where the church is sited for the maximum convenience of the family, at Tardebigge the great house, Hewell Grange, is well away while the church forms part of a little unit of smaller buildings which used to house an alehouse and now includes the village school. Entirely to be expected is the specific area in the churchyard for members of the Windsor family who lived at Hewell Grange, an area in front of the main west entrance neatly fenced off with manicured trees. Inside are two plots, one to the Plymouth family, the other to the relations by marriage of a nineteenth-century Lord Windsor, themselves of high rank.

The Plymouth area, the plainer of the two, contains the grave of young William Windsor, destined to be vicar but, sadly, killed in a railway accident in 1857. The curate who had arrived two years earlier merely to keep the seat warm for him was invited to stay on. No-one could have envisaged that the young man, Rev Charles Dickins, would remain until 1917 — 62 years vicar of Tardebigge. He is buried with his wife and clergyman son nearby.

The other enclosure, its topiary shaped into elegant arches,

Topiaried privacy for the Paget family at Tardebigge

contains three gravestones, plain in appearance, exotic in detail, to the Paget family whose daughter had married into the family of the Earls of Plymouth. Sir Augustus Berkeley Paget had quite an eventful diplomatic career being in Paris when Louis Napoleon overthrew the government to found the Second Empire, at Copenhagen when Prussia overran parts of Denmark in the early stages of the campaign to create Germany, and then in Rome in 1867 to see the first King of Italy enter and claim that country's independence. With typical British understatement he is quoted as saying that in his work 'considerable tact had been required'. Sir Augustus's wife may hold the record in the county for the number of letters needed to give her name and lineage: 'Walburga Ehrengarda Helena daughter of Charles Frederic Antony Count v Hohenthal & Loida Emilia Countess Neidhardt v Greisenam'. Before she married she was lady-in-waiting to the Princess Royal, later Empress of Germany. The stone that separates man and wife, to Lieutenant Colonel Victor Paget, could not differ more. It simply says: 'The kind are cheerful and serene like travellers that are going towards home'.

In stark contrast to the opulent say-it-all approach to memorials are those modest, briefly worded stones to people of outstanding achievement whose fame lives on, whose names are amongst the best known of all. On the edge of Birmingham a plain gravestone in Lickey churchyard records that Herbert 1st Baron Austin of Longbridge was born 8 November 1886 and died 23 May 1941, and Helen, Lady Austin, was born 23 October 1866 and died 24 May 1942. There is no hint that here is a pioneering car manufacturer whose vehicles achieved for him worldwide fame from the enormous factory almost within sight. His first engineering work had been for his uncle in Australia where he had gone for some experience and maybe his enthusiasm for a petrol-powered means of transport grew from the long journeys he had to do there for the sheepshearing company he managed. His modest grave is in sharp contrast to the nearby flamboyant stone, complete with angel, which commemorates a now forgotten nineteenth-century clergyman. In fairness to the clerical gentleman it must be said that showy memorials and laudatory verse are not the twentieth century's tastes; but modest headstones were being erected to the great before that gentleman died.

At West Malvern, for instance, there is a very plain gravestone near the war memorial in St James' churchyard whose inscription could not be simpler: 'Peter Mark Roget FRS MD died 1869 aged 91'. Yet this is the man whose sheer genius has raised to universal by-word status the unlikely combination of a French surname and a Greek noun. He was not a Worcestershire man but a Scot who was visiting Malvern at the time of his death and he had devised his scheme as a young busy doctor to help him improve his powers of expression. Years later he developed this into what he described as his 'classed catalogue of words'. Roget's *Thesaurus of English Words and Phrases, Classified and Arranged So As to Facilitate the Expression of Ideas and Assist in Literary Composition* was immediately and amazingly successful, never out of print since its publication 140 years ago. It has been revised, modified and remodelled but retains its original structure.

The waters of Malvern and its beautiful position have drawn many to end their days in the shadow of the hills, the most famous of these Edward Elgar; and he was born only a few miles along the road at Lower Broadheath. He lived for many years in Malvern and is buried at St Wulstan's Roman Catholic Church, Malvern Wells. Like Roget's his stone is surprisingly plain, a flat slab with just his surname which lies at the foot of a headstone to his wife who predeceased him. It is a modest memorial, in an apparently little tended churchyard, for the Master of the King's Musick and arguably the county's most famous son whose love for this area inspired his greatest music.

The graves of Austin, Roget and Elgar may be unadorned but their household names are likely to attract the churchyard visitor. Other simple stones may go unnoticed because the names on them mean nothing to the late-twentieth century reader; but in their day and in their sphere they achieved much. A case in point is the red sandstone memorial to the Griffiths family, at Ribbesford, father George, mother and two sons who died before their parents. Nothing remarkable here. But in his time Griffiths must have driven numerous people mad as he singlemindedly laid into one after another of the county's schools, village, cathedral and especially the endowed grammar schools, many of which were in a deplorable state and misusing funds by excluding those very children originally meant to

Worcestershire's most famous son: the simple gravestone to Sir Edward and Lady Elgar at St Wulstan's, Malvern Wells

benefit from them. Griffiths, a corn merchant from a comfortable Birmingham family, travelled extensively, often on horseback; and he was fearless in his condemnation of narrow, irrelevant curricula, apathetic teachers and uncooperative trustees, arguing always for the development of popular education for the children of the poor. He was absolutely right as a reading of his books (available in local libraries) will confirm.

A large tombstone to Benjamin Maund and his wife, near the east end of St John's, Bromsgrove, is another that will almost certainly go unnoticed, unless, that is, the visitor has first gone into the church and spied on the south side of the chancel two memorial windows to Maund's mother, wife and second son, John, whose distinguished medical career included the founding of the Women's Hospital in Melbourne. John has a handsome tombstone, a feature on a tour of Melbourne's large cemetery. Back in his home church the window has the wrong year of death for him which is balanced by another bit of misleading information on his parents' grave outside. For despite what it seems Benjamin is not buried alongside his wife but in Brading on the Isle of Wight where he died in retirement. He was a man of many parts, a bookseller, with a business in the High Street; a printer and publisher; and a self-taught botanist who took a great interest in all the developing sciences, gathered plants from all around the world, conducted all sorts of experiments in his large garden and was the proud possessor of a microscope before either St Bartholomew's Hospital or the Natural History Department of the British Museum had one. Amazingly, from a small obscure country town he managed to secure the cooperation of the leading professors of botany of his day and to employ highly skilled artists to illustrate his horticultural and botanical works. His first publication *The Botanic Garden* was of exceptional quality, still regarded by today's experts as head and shoulders above almost all the rest of similar offerings. Through

this and later works Maund achieved an international reputation
and is said to have turned down a knighthood. Forgotten now
but a man of great distinction a century and a half ago.

At Catshill the absence of a body in one part of the churchyard
is much more obvious, a case not so much of who is but who
isn't there; for the ashes of the most distinguished member of
the Housman family, poet and classical scholar, Alfred Edward,
lie not among his relatives in that parish where he was born and
christened and spent his teenage years but in Ludlow in
Shropshire. Housman admitted his sentimental feeling for that
county whose 'hills were our western horizon' and confessed to
having written six of the Shropshire poems before he had set
foot there. (Nor is it certain that his acquaintanceship with it
ever became more than superficial.) But two generations of his
family are buried together. His grandfather's memorial is a very
large gaunt cross mounted on a plinth and records in ringing
nineteenth-century tones that we may find slightly histrionic the
fact that he was the church's first vicar, entrusted with 'this
church, this God's acre, this parish'.

Perhaps 'A E' wanted to take his final rest well away from his
relatives: the adjoining graves hint at some of the tensions at
play in that large family. The poet's stepmother, Lucy Agnes,
made sure that when her husband died he was not buried with
his first wife, the mother of his seven children, but in a new
grave into which she herself could be lowered in due course; and
she gave clear instructions on the manner of this 'lowering' — in
an 'elm box without any shape ... with charcoal to assist decay'
and containing locks of her mother's hair and her husband's
beard and the coat of a dog that had died years before. Somehow
it is a melancholy corner for a family which produced the varied
talents of Alfred, Laurence and Clemence.

Benjamin Maund is not the only bookseller to have achieved
fame. Another was George Nicholson who is buried in
Stourport. Nicholson was a Yorkshireman who first set up

business in Bradford where he attracted attention by publishing inexpensive editions of books which led consequently to their wider readership; but it was as a county bookseller in Stourport that he effected a real revolution in the style and appearance of pocket volumes and fostered the popularity of well printed handy editions of favourite authors. He deliberately set out to employ the best artists and engravers for the frontispieces and portraits in the books he printed — people like Thomas Bewick — and his refined work was soon copied by the main booksellers in London. As well as a printer and publisher he was the author of a number of books and tracts aimed at the poorer members of society and he might also have been the first to write about vegetarian cookery for he was a convinced vegetarian and wrote enthusiastically about the cultivation and use of vegetables.

Yet another bookseller and, like Maund, a self-taught botanist, while not achieving the same measure of fame, made a great contribution during his lifetime to the quality of life in Worcestershire. Edwin Lees was born in Worcester in 1800, and after a modest education was apprenticed to a printer. But the great passion of his life had already taken a firm hold. From a boy he was interested in his natural surroundings and was still only in his twenties when he founded the Worcestershire Literary and Scientific Institute and was able to set up in the High Street as a master printer and bookseller. Four years later he was one of three founding members of the Worcestershire Natural History Society which had its own museum and library on the site of the present Odeon Cinema.

But Lees must have kept hard at his daily business because he was able to sell out and retire before he was 40 and devote the rest of his long life to studying and writing principally about the botany of Worcestershire. He was particularly interested in the form of brambles and is commemorated by the *Rubus Leesii* named by a Cambridge professor following its discovery by Lees in Devon. Lees died in Worcester in 1887 but is buried with his first wife in Upper Pendock, a redundant church now, standing in the middle of a field approached by a rough path, with fine views of the Malverns but right next to the noisy M50. Lees' great friend, Rev W S Symonds, rector and Pendock's lord of the manor, had been buried there only a month before and both funerals, according to Elgar's brother-in-law, required the large numbers attending to walk in worse conditions than they met on their naturalist tours.

The headstone stands between two cypress trees, the huge one behind the stone the subject of a request: 'Spare the Tree planted by his Direction'; the smaller which nestles against it over the grave was planted in his memory over 40 years later by the Malvern Naturalists' Field Club. The Worcestershire Naturalists' Club he helped found is still in existence nearly 150 years later.

It is true that Worcestershire has not produced writers in the

Frances Ridley Havergal's beautifully sited grave at Astley

same league as those of neighbouring Warwickshire, but authors like Layamon, Langland, Housman and Francis Brett Young have certainly contributed to our literary life. One who is still 'read' regularly is hymnwriter Frances Ridley Havergal born at Astley, the youngest child of the rector. She lived the fairly uneventful life of a clergyman's unmarried daughter — governess, doer of good works, climbing in the Alps and labouring for the evangelical wing of the Church of England. She was an exceptionally bright child who enjoyed singing and was composing verse at seven. Her hymns are still included in the latest collections.

The family grave at Astley, where her father, mother and stepmother are also buried, is in a tranquil spot surrounded by fields and rolling hills. Her funeral was neither tranquil nor sombre for Frances had requested that it be a joyous occasion. She died near Swansea and a young man who witnessed the cortege from Stourport station to Astley later described it in his memoirs of life in the Teme Valley: 'The sight riveted me. It was not a funeral cortege with nodding plumes ... but instead a car of triumph, gaily dressed with wreaths of laurel, and on the coffin itself a golden star of Banksia roses ...'. The attendants wore white gloves, waistcoats and buttonholes to express her confidence that death was for her the triumphal entry into God's presence.

In strong contrast to the modest Havergal tomb is a giant of a memorial at Himbleton, a cross mounted on a stepped octagonal base, in all some 20 feet high. The sheer size and position of the monument, surrounded by tall conifers on the edge of the churchyard, immediately attracts the attention; but a closer inspection reveals very little. It is in memory of Sir Douglas Galton who died in 1899. Sir Douglas was buried at nearby Hadzor where his family held the lordship of the manor; but he must have wished he hadn't been, for he was a strong advocate of cremation at a time when the process, though legal, horrified

Sir Douglas Galton's towering cross at Himbleton

most people. Educated at Rugby during Dr Arnold's time, he did the decent thing and entered the army. But he became interested in the problems of what was then called 'sanitary science' — not something, clearly, his family wanted inscribing on his massive memorial: they stuck to the solitary fact that he was the second son of the lord of the manor. Sir Douglas appears to have had the sort of career which called for ingenuity, a strong investigative turn of mind and probably at times a good stomach, covering the sanitary problems relating to military hospitals, preservation of the Thames embankment, laying of the Atlantic telephone cable, the use of iron in railway structures and, commendably, the importance of higher education for women.

In Sir Charles Bell's case it's the fulsomeness of the epitaph on a plaque inside the church rather than the magnitude of the stone which is noteworthy. Part of it will convey the tone:

... who after unfolding with unrivalled sagacity, patience and success
the wonderful structure of our mortal bodies esteemed lightly of his
greatest discoveries except only as they tended to impress himself
and others with a deeper sense of the wisdom and ineffable goodness
of the Almighty Creator.

But Bell was a most important person in the development of
medicine, whose achievements deserve to be better known. He
discovered the distinct functions of nerves, the two kinds of
nerves necessary for muscles, the motor nerve to excite action,
the sensory nerve to convey the sense of that action. This work
culminated in the publication of *The Nervous System of the
Human Body* in 1830. He was a celebrated figure in London but
never really liked living there and in 1836 returned to his native
city, Edinburgh, as professor of surgery. Like Roget he was
merely visiting Worcestershire when he died in 1842 and is
buried somewhere in Hallow churchyard. Unfortunately, his
gravestone is no longer there.

In a number of churchyards around the county are stones
whose shape suggests a body wrapped in bands inside, a full-
length rounded stone often with a cross or leaves carved on the
top and with rectangular ends shaped to look like footstools.
There are three in a row at Broadway as though a family long
ago bought a job lot. Inscriptions have often faded but not that
of one of the greatest Victorian explorers in East Africa, Sir
Samuel Baker, who is buried at Grimley. This must have been a
quiet backwater to retire to after his adventurous life. Born in
London in 1821, the son of a merchant with interests in the
West Indies, he began to wander soon after his marriage — but
he took his wife and two brothers with him to start an estate in
Ceylon where they stayed for nine years. Sadly, his wife died
and to take his mind off his loss he started to travel in eastern
Europe and in Turkey where he met a kindred spirit and
married for the second time. Fascinated by the story of John

Speke and the search for the source of the Nile, the couple went to Egypt and sailed up the Nile, mapping, hunting and exploring tributaries high in the Sudan. His greatest discovery (his wife was there but comatose in a sedan chair and near to death) was the Albert Nyanza lake out of which flowed the White Nile. Mrs Baker recovered and two years later her husband was knighted. He was appointed Governor General of Equatorial Africa and following that masterminded a railway from the Danube to the Black Sea before coming to rest near the banks of another great river, the Severn.

6 A sudden end

 There cannot be a churchyard in the county that does not hold below its surface the remains of those whose deaths were far from natural. In many instances the gravestones, where they existed at all, have disappeared or are no longer readable; while others, though still standing, give no hint that the deceased's passing might have been anything but peaceful. But, as well as those already mentioned in other connections, there still exist a number of memorials in Worcestershire churchyards which tell us clearly that these were no ordinary departures. Some very clearly indeed.

> James Davies of Worcester Constabulary, murdered whilst in the execution of his duty in the early morning of February 28 1885 aged 33 leaving an example of faithful service to his native country.

Davis had gone on duty at 10 o'clock on the Friday evening, met up with the Wythall policeman three hours later — as was the practice then — and at 2.15 on the Saturday morning had set off to meet the Alvechurch policeman at Rowney Green. The latter, though, was at home ill; so it was not until 8.30 that a Rowney Green farmer came across a body lying face down in a pool of

Murdered while on duty: PC James Davies, Beoley

blood in the middle of the road near Weatheroak Hill. The farmer recognised Davies and the Wythall policeman was sent for. He supervised the removal of the body to the shed of a wheelwright named Simpson, about half a mile away at the crossroads.

It was clear that a desperate struggle had taken place at that lonely, narrow part of the road; and it was soon discovered that six fowl had been stolen in the vicinity that same night. Suspicion immediately fell on Moses Shrimpton and accounts in the newspaper of the time read like a Victorian melodrama rather than the real Victorian tragedy it was. Shrimpton was a well-known fowl-stealer, just out of gaol in fact for having been caught the previous year on Solihull station with sixteen of the creatures about his person. He was also known to be violent, bad-tempered and a heavy drinker. And he looked the part: small, strong and shabby. No-one was surprised when a large two-bladed pocket knife was discovered in the skirt of his lover,

Mary Moreton, in their digs in Birmingham; when his clothes, including his billycock, were found to have blood on them; and when Moreton tried to sell PC Davies's watch. One fact emerges from contemporary accounts which is rather surprising. Shrimpton was not only smaller but nearly twice the age of Davies. He came from Astwood Bank, a worker in the needle trade before taking to a life of crime; so presumably he knew this part of Worcestershire well. But on the night in question he must have exerted great strength to resist arrest.

Moses Shrimpton and Mary Moreton were both hung. PC James Davies, father of four, was buried at Beoley with great crowds in attendance.

Much less clear-cut was a murder at the isolated village of Berrow, the other end of the county, a century earlier. It is commemorated by a stone set into the outside wall of the church just to the right of the porch.

Tablet to the Gummary family, murdered at Berrow two centuries ago

> Under the stone beneath this tablet lie the remains of Edward
> Gummary, Elizabeth his wife and Ann their daughter, who were
> cruelly murdered at the cottage known as the murder house in the
> parish of Berrow on the night of May 7 1780.

In fact a fourth person was murdered there, Thomas Sheen,
Elizabeth's brother who had the misfortune to be staying the
night. Gummary's neighbours heard strange noises in the night
and on investigating found Mr and Mrs Gummary on the floor
and nine-year-old Ann on the bed and in the adjoining bedroom
Thomas Sheen on a bed, all four brutally hacked to death. No
money had been stolen, 'nor doth it appear the house was
plundered', records *Berrow's Worcester Journal*; and neighbours
confirmed that the family had been an honest and industrious
one, 'very harmless, inoffensive people, and not given to
quarrel'. So why were they murdered? Several theories were put
forward, the most likely — interestingly enough, passed down
from one generation to the next and offered by present-day
villagers — that Edward Gummary had informed on a sheep
stealer who had taken his ultimate revenge.

There are links with the county's most famous murders in two
mid-Worcestershire churchyards. At Droitwich (St Peter de
Witton) there is a rather nondescript ledger tomb near the
southern boundary which informs us that buried there are the
bodies of Catherine Banks of Oddingley and Captain Samuel
Evans 'whose name is connected with double murder at
Oddingley in the year 1806'. The language is necessarily
cautious since no-one was ever convicted; but who decided to
mention it at all? Surely not Evans himself who was almost
certainly the organiser of both murders. At Salwarpe the plain
headstone to Thomas Clewes gives nothing away about his
involvement in the same affair though he it was who finally
explained what had happened years before.

In the early years of the last century Rev George Parker

decided he wanted to increase the tithes paid to him by the parishioners of the small village of Oddingley, tucked away down a lane off the main Worcester road. Naturally his flock refused. So he built a barn in order to collect tithes in kind, thus reverting to the former method of payment, and demanded that the parishioners should foot the bill for the new building. Discontent rose and a conspiracy, not terribly subtle, was hatched to get rid of the 'pestilent priest'. Towards evening on 24 June 1806, Midsummer Day, Parker was shot while out in his fields.

A man called Richard Hemming was immediately sought and a reward offered for his capture; for Hemming, a Droitwich carpenter, had been seen lurking in the fields next to the glebe and someone claimed to have recognised him running away from the scene of the crime. It was known from the start however that certain local farmers had probably organised the whole business, that Hemming was merely a tool; and subsequently Captain Samuel Evans, gentleman farmer and magistrate, John Barnett, a farmer, and a farrier called Taylor were arrested — and promptly released for lack of evidence.

Twenty-four years passed before a macabre discovery revealed the depth to which the conspirators had sunk. The new owner of Netherwood Farm decided to restore a dilapidated old barn. Hemming's skeleton was unearthed in the process, finally giving the lie to the general conclusion that he must have escaped to America; and Thomas Clewes, former owner of the farm, was arrested.

After a couple of days in gaol Clewes confessed that Hemming, hired to kill the parson, had then been lured to his death by Captain Evans, his adopted son George Banks and Taylor, the latter battering him to death and burying him in Clewes' barn. Banks and John Barnett were immediately arrested, but despite their obvious guilt all three were released for by this time Evans and Taylor were both dead and as the law

The peaceful churchyard at Oddingley, once the centre of a double murder

then stood accessories to a murder could not be tried after the death of the principal suspect. Their release was celebrated at Oddingley with beer, tobacco and a ringing of the church bells. Clewes, who had witnessed a murder and been bribed to keep silent, lived on to the great age of 93; but much of that time seems to have been unhappy. Within a few years of the murders his farm had gone downhill and he was forced to sell it and work there as a labourer.

Nothing much changes though and, like today, the vast majority of unnatural deaths in the past were not the result of personally inflicted violence but of accidents at home, at work or on the highway. An example of a very early motoring accident is to be found in Cofton Hackett's extensive churchyard on the very edge of the Lickey Hills where there are a number of gravestones to the Myatt family, including a very ornate and huge one, several yards across and twice the length. It is in memory of Arthur Myatt who died 25 July 1913 from 'injuries received in a tragic motor car accident on the 19th inst. by which two other young men were killed'.

It happened on a summer's day when 'five Birmingham gentlemen' were travelling to Bromsgrove in a small Humber driven by George Totman. A few miles north of Bromsgrove on a bend near Chadwich the car skidded for no apparent reason and all five were thrown out. Totman died on the spot and one of his passengers shortly after. Myatt lingered for a few days. The verdict was accidental death but the jury made a statement about the deathtrap of a corner and the coroner agreed to write to the clerk to the county council about it. How familiar it all sounds 80 years later. And had the accident never taken place how many of these young men would have survived the coming armed conflict?

In the early days of the railway era there were a number of fatal accidents. Some of these, including the two most famous, have already been mentioned in a previous chapter; but there were others, one of them not nearly as straightforward as the headstone suggests:

> In memory of WILLIAM CREUZE, B.A. of St Johns College, Cambs., and Chief Engineer of Locomotives on the Birmingham & Gloucester Railway, who died through injuries received accidentally on that railway April 8th 1841 aged 31.

William Creuze, gentleman and graduate, was in charge of the locomotive works at Aston Fields in which Rutherford and Scaife worked. It was a very difficult period indeed: the building itself, quite inadequate, had been put up at breakneck speed to be ready for the opening of the Bromsgrove to Cheltenham section of the line in June 1840; the equipment assembled was primitive; the staff were largely untrained; and the workload was frightening. Creuze was probably too sensitive a soul for this work and soon despairing at the hopelessness of it all took to drink. Rutherford was the one who kept things going through sheer determination but his replacement was a different kettle of fish, a man of much lower standards. After a drinking bout up at the Malt Shovel in Vigo, Creuze and several others were returning on the 'Boston' in the early hours when one of the many botched jobs gave way. Creuze was too drunk to move, scalded to death as steam sprayed over the footplate; but his death at least served a purpose, for the inquest opened up the can of worms and the railway company realised the need for sweeping changes to be made.

Before the car and the train it was shanks's pony that got you around or, if you were a little more prosperous, a horse. In the north-west side of St John's churchyard in Bromsgrove is a largish headstone to John English 'Veterinary Surgeon of this Town who died suddenly by a fall from his Horse on 18th of August 1832 aged 32'. It would be reasonable to assume from the information given that this was yet another accident that could be put down to the appalling state of the roads. But this was summer, the best time for travelling, so perhaps there was another reason for the fall.

Ironically, it was because it was summer that the accident occurred at all. John English was riding over to Tardebigge, possibly in connection with his job as Veterinary Surgeon to the Worcestershire Yeomanry Cavalry, when his horse took fright at some children, their arms full of wheat. Had they been shouting and laughing perhaps on that late summer day? Certainly the vet was taken unawares and thrown violently to the ground. His injuries were so severe that he died the same day. Five days later he was buried with military honours and to the sound of the regimental band, his funeral attended by the Earl of Plymouth, Lord Aston and nearly every member of the two Tardebigge troops.

By far the most curious deaths in the county took place in the most unlikely places: on a cricket field in the village of

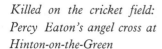

Killed on the cricket field: Percy Eaton's angel cross at Hinton-on-the-Green

Honeybourne on the Gloucestershire border, and in the magnificent Perpendicular tower of St John's, Bromsgrove.

Percy Eaton was a popular young farm bailiff, son of a well-known farming family, and a key all-round athlete. He played in several football teams, was a good rider, a fine shot and a very competent rower; and not long before his death he had taken to cricket.

In the late afternoon of the day in question (strangely, 18 August again) Percy was at the crease, helping the Honeybourne cricket team to beat rivals Hampton. Perhaps he was thinking how good life was — soon to be married, lots of friends, a responsible job and a winning team — when he prepared to face the next ball. The bowler was the Fladbury curate, Rev Frank Venables, and he delivered a full pitched ball. As Percy struck it the ball flew off the edge of his bat and onto his neck near his right ear. He fell to the ground and a doctor was immediately summoned from Evesham. He had been dead some time when the doctor arrived, his neck dislocated, the inquest concluded, by the sudden jerk as the ball hit him. The inquest was a sad affair: everyone knew that no-one was to blame, a fact stressed several times. But it was little comfort to the curate. Percy Eaton's memorial, in the form of an angel cross, stands in the churchyard at Hinton-on-the-Green.

Nothing could be more Gothic than the demise of John Rose who died in 1879. If the account appeared in a Victorian novel it would be credited nowadays only with indulgence. The Rose family's service to the parish has already been remarked upon. John had taken over from his father in 1869 as sexton, clerk, registrar and gravedigger and on Saturday 22 March he was busy as usual getting the church ready for the Sunday services. Some time between 7 and 8 o'clock he climbed up to the belfry to wind the clock and close the windows, turned, and in the darkness fell through one of the trap doors which was regularly raised to help disperse the smoke given off by the heating system. Some parishioners reported hearing the sound of the small bell at twenty minutes to eight and it was assumed Rose had either fallen across the bell rope or, since it was found to be broken in two, clutched at it as he fell.

It was unusual that on that day John Rose did not have the help of his nephew Joseph, a nineteen-year-old who lived with him and normally performed the duty of winding the clock; and it is when the very full newspaper report turns to Joseph's evidence that there creeps in the mildest of question marks about the tragedy. Joseph, a pupil teacher, had excused himself that day in order to study for his exam. Was it the unexpected sound of the bell that suddenly reminded him that he had left the trap door open? In any event he seems to have run to the church to warn his uncle, arriving only seconds after the accident. He lifted his uncle onto a seat and talked to him; but only after three or four minutes, when John Rose appeared to die, did he fetch a doctor. Joseph seems to have been questioned rather closely about his assertion that his uncle had definitely been up in the belfry — who else could have closed the windows and wound the clock? And the writer of the report points out that Joseph was the only witness to be called: no evidence was taken from Dr Wood who told the newspaper he had found the deceased quite sensible and wanting 'to walk home'.

The verdict was accidental death; an iron grating was put over the trap door; John Rose was buried with great ceremony; and within three weeks young Joseph Rose, with the support of the vicar, churchwardens and schoolmaster, was appointed clerk and sexton, a suggestion that it should be for an initial twelve months only duly dismissed.

Index

Worcestershire place names mentioned in the text